D1486376

The Coach House
Cats

The Coach House
Cats

Marilyn Edwards

MARILYN EDWARDS

ILLUSTRATED BY

PETER WARNER

HODDER &
STOUGHTON

British Library Cataloguing in Publication Data
A record for this book is available from the British Library

ISBN-10: 0 340 90904 8
ISBN-13: 978 0340 90904 1

Typeset in Gaudy by Avon Dataset Ltd,
Bidford-on-Avon, Warwickshire

Printed and bound in Great Britain by
Clays Ltd, St Ives plc

The paper used in this book is a natural recyclable product
made from wood grown in sustainable forests.
The hard coverboard is recycled.

Hodder & Stoughton
A Division of Hodder Headline Ltd
338 Euston Road
London NW1 3BH
www.madaboutbooks.com

To Geoffrey Moorhouse, with love

CHAPTER 1

Richard's eyes crinkle up with glee and he beams at me wickedly.

'Oooh, small kittens can be drowned quite easily in watering cans, can't they?' I grab my neck, hand on hand, in mock horror and grin back at him, ruefully. Michael and I are about to take a walk in the Cumbrian hills on this brash breezy November day and we have just told our friend and neighbour the news that Fannie, my beloved tortie queen, is pregnant. Richard is well aware that my Achilles' heel is the cats and takes every opportunity presented to him to tease me about them. As we take our leave with the intention of walking up the road, he turns towards his own driveway, but as he does so he calls out over his shoulder:

'When are the kittens due, by the way?'

'Twenty-third of January,' I call back.

'Ah, that's still within the shooting season,' he laughs, disappearing behind our dividing wall before I can think of a suitable reply. As we walk away I find myself grinning broadly; Richard is at heart one big softie.

Fannie has been different since the first day that she returned from her visit to her boyfriend Zimmy, an apricot Oriental stud who lives over in East Lancashire. It is just eleven days since she was mated and she is showing small signs already that some biological change has taken place. She is sleeping far more than is her normal pattern, but when she is awake she is busy all day long, trotting round the entire house, looking, looking, looking. I have never seen her so distracted. It is as if she has lost something and she must find it, but I know, early though it is, in reality she is trying to find a nesting place. She has been sleeping in the bottom of the wardrobe in the spare bedroom for much of the time. She no longer lies next to her sister, Titus, but perhaps this is a necessary form of burgeoning independence. Titus is rampantly on heat at the moment and Pushkin, the Russian Blue whom I had hoped would father kittens with one or other of the girls, continues, fastidiously, to avoid her advances.

When I hold Fannie on my shoulder she is more clingy and purrful than normal, but that might be to compensate for her changing relationship with her sister. She seems to ignore Pushkin completely.

A date is in the diary for two hysterectomies and a castration for, respectively, Fannie, Titus (male name but female cat) and Pushkin, to be performed by our local vet, Gerard, in just over a month's time, but Fannie's longed-for pregnancy will now of necessity reduce the number of patients to two. A friend fervently advises me to consider not spaying Titus at this time, as she believes that it could cause Titus to show aggression towards Fannie, who might then miscarry. I phone the long-suffering Gerard and ask him what I should do and he reckons that spaying Titus and Pushkin is fine, although he does express some concern that Titus is on one of her semi-permanent heats, but we agree to stick with the arrangement and I quietly offer up a prayer that all will be well. I deeply regret that Titus will not be able to bear one litter, but Gerard, when last he saw her, recommended that, as a cat who has endured separate operations on each of her back legs in turn to correct luxating patellae, she should not be encouraged to reproduce.

Since moving into our little eyrie in the county of

Westmorland,[1] it seems to me that the cats' lives are now so eventful that, were they capable of such a thought process, they should see that the move they had originally hated so much was in reality a good thing. It is probable, however, that the three cats have no

---

[1] Otherwise known as Cumbria, but many local people continue proudly to refer to it by its earlier and more romantic name.

perception of what life in Moon Cottage was like compared with their new life in the Coach House. Their new life means that now, for two hours at a time, they go outside freely to roam; they have the stimuli of the smells and sounds borne to them on the country winds; they regularly experience the thrill of the chase and, more rarely, kill; all this they have, while I quietly torture myself about their newly increased vulnerability.

🐾 🐾 🐾

The strangest thing has just happened and I am filled with remorse, and yet I am uncertain what it is that I should have done to prevent it. It has been raining on and off for most of the day but the rain finally stops at around 8 p.m. and, as I look out of the window of the conservatory, through the gloom I see large dark clouds scudding across the sky heavy with more rain. It is a dark, dank night and the tang of autumn hangs in the air. I open the front door to go out to the freezer in the shed to bring in some fish for supper and, as I move forward to cross the threshold, I see Titus speeding across the tiles of the conservatory floor towards me and as she reaches me, in spite of my best endeavours to stop her, she shoots through the door and out into the garden. Although I am now letting the cats out more and more during daylight hours, I draw the line once it is dark for the dangers that lie in wait in such deep countryside as this for so unworldly a crew as these three cats frighten me too much. I shout out harshly: 'Come here, Titus, at once!' She ignores me completely. Well, not completely, in truth, she runs away as fast as she can so that as I try to stop her, I end up chasing her. She comes to a halt at the bench under the seven giant Scots pines and as I reach her I grab her by the scruff of her neck. She wrenches herself away from me and as she does so she makes the most extraordinary howling, screeching sort of noise, the like of which I have never heard her utter in her entire life. Although I feel sure I can barely have hurt her, she hisses at me with either fear or loathing or both – I stand helplessly by as she runs into the furthest corner of the garden, amid bushes and trees and where there is not the earthly possibility of my catching her if she doesn't wish it. I walk dejectedly back into the house and shut the door. Fannie is there waiting, presumably having heard her sister's ear-shattering protests, and miaows several times to be let out which I resist. I tell Michael what has happened but I try to persuade him to leave her to get over whatever it is that upset her, believing that she will come back on her own in due time. Michael, however, insists on trying to comfort her himself. I hear him calling her but she remains hidden in the dark. He lets out Fannie, who disappears briefly but quite quickly reappears on her own with no sign of her sister in tow. Fannie comes back into the house with me and I shut the door again. I start to cook the supper and try to persuade myself that all will be well and Titus will be fine and will get over it, but I am completely

perplexed at whatever it was that upset her so much. Yes, she was cross that I was attempting to curtail her dash for freedom but the screech was so strong that it was as if she thought I was strangling her. I finally can't bear it a second longer and go out into the garden and then the field at the back and whistle repeatedly. If she is within a quarter of a mile of the house she must be able to hear me, but there is still no sign of her. She has now been out about an hour. I turn to come back into the house and as I do so I hear a scuffling noise from the bushes by the ashbin and Titus slightly shiftily appears out of the gloom. I call her and pick her up. She stiffens in my arms and there is no purring, but she doesn't scratch or wriggle to get free, so in some sense a truce is established.

Later on that night Michael makes an observation with a note of sad questioning in his voice:

'I have been thinking, and you know, you must agree, Titus is the most balanced of the three cats. She is the least neurotic, she shows affection the most easily of all of them – if you think about it she is always the most responsive, and she really is the least nervous.' He pauses for a little while, and then he adds, 'It makes her being so odd with you even stranger!'

'Well yes, but she *was* odd and we'll just have to live with it,' I retort between gritted teeth. But, of course, I am tormented with guilt about Titus whom I never love enough, although I do spend time with her, consciously loving her, to compensate. You can't manufacture love, you can only try to give as much as you can, and to be nice if all else fails.

CHAPTER 2

Right through the long hot summer and now the damp blustery autumn of this first year of our new life in Cumbria every move we have made, every penny we have spent, has been overshadowed by our fears that if we are not able to sell Moon Cottage soon we will no longer be able to afford the two mortgages and the day will shortly dawn when we must put our new home, the Coach House, back on the market, on the grounds that in a tourist beauty spot we stand a better chance of a quick sale than in the commuter lands of the Home Counties.

However, the cats remain untouched by this for

the moment and Fannie continues to flourish and occupies herself incessantly around the house hunting for her ideal nest. I am amazed at how much food she is eating and the variety of what she eats. She is now prepared to eat food she would not formerly have touched and I have started to feed her kitten food when the others aren't around, as it is higher in nutrients and good for a pregnant queen. As I watch the cats I mull over the complication of the bond that humans feel for the animals who share their lives. I am still haunted by the hurt I feel I cause to Titus because I do not love her enough in *her* mind, or is that in truth in *my* mind? I find this diary entry, which I submit unedited, guilty as charged:

Fannie jumps into one of the big boxes on the bedroom floor and looks out over the high side of it, with just her eyes showing, which has the effect on me of melting my inner core, not just my emotions but it feels to me, as I write, my whole being.

When Fannie peeks at me over the top of the box

I think the reason I dissolve is that all I can see of her are her two pert ears and her adorable, large, liquid eyes. I can't see her nose or her whiskers or her mouth and indeed when I do reach over to look at her whole face, the bottom half is comparatively expressionless, the intensity of her expression is conveyed solely through her eyes in the manner of a veiled woman and it's utterly beguiling.

Throughout all of this anguishing somehow Pushkin does not generate any of these anxieties within me. He and I know and understand each other well and it is very straightforward. He comes to me when he needs love (and sometimes he will go to Michael, although Pushkin is more of a one-person cat than the others) and otherwise he sleeps. He remains nervous when he is outside although he does love going out, but at the slightest sound of a vehicle or even a strong wind he comes racing inside. Pushkin is a very beautiful wuss-puss. Of all the cats it is Pushkin who most shares my fear of road traffic and its possible effect on the cats.

My heart was broken when Otto, the mother of Fannie and Titus, was killed on the road outside our house. When I started to write the book about her life and was talking about the grief I felt at her death, my bookseller friend David told me the sad story of his beloved moggy, Jack, who one day went missing from his terrace house in Lancaster. David says that he will never forget the anguish that he went through on the days following that first night that Jack didn't come home.

'You imagine the worst, and you almost want to know the worst so that there is nothing terrible left to discover.'

After phoning the vet and speaking to other folk in the street he establishes that on the night of Jack's disappearance a cat is discovered at the end of his long street, dead, having been run over in the main road. The vet tries to reassure David that the cat is not Jack, but eventually – Jack never reappears – David convinces himself that it is too much of a coincidence that a cat with exactly Jack's colouration has died the same night that David first misses his little cat. In his reluctance to con-template the death of Jack, it is two days before

David finally drags himself to the vet's, intending to inspect the corpse, but by then the cat has been cremated and so, with a heavy heart, he returns home none the wiser. I so empathise with him and all those other bereaved cat owners who will never know for certain what has happened to their loved feline companion. And now, three years later, having returned North at last, I decide to seek out David on his home turf. When I arrive he has to introduce me to no less than *three* significant-other male companions. One, his human partner Peter, is a warm and gracious man who is just enchanting, and the other two, by whom I am no less captivated, are a pair of feline brothers named Merlin and Gizmo. Merlin is long and lean and muscular and reminds me, exactly, of Pushkin in his build, his shape, his sleekness and the conformation of his ears. He must surely have been fathered by a cat with some Russian Blue in him, I quietly ponder. He is a beautiful dark grey, almost black, and his eyes are the striking amber of Titus's. He has a strong otherworldly look to him. Gizmo is altogether different. He's a white-bibbed, white-stockinged tabby with an adorable pink nose and he is a hopeless flirt. He is also indubitably fat. As this patently applies to me as well, it is with some hypocrisy that I cry out:

'Good heavens, Gizmo! How on earth did you get to be that shape?' I hear Peter laugh, but David rather defensively says:

'It's not his fault. He's an indoors cat, and simply can't get enough exercise.' David is too much of a gentleman to ask me if that is also my problem. On full investigation of the whats and wherefores of the domestic arrangements of this very male household I discover that Merlin is the shy, heat-loving, purring fave of Dave and that Gizmo is the wayward, engaging passion of Peter's life whose day starts with a disarmingly familiar cuddle with his precious Gizmo to mine with Fannie.

'Ah,' I find myself murmuring indulgently, 'the morning cuddle, I understand, I understand.' But I quickly discover that the ritual in this household is significantly more complex than mine. There are two fish tanks – one upstairs and one downstairs. The fish tank upstairs 'belongs' to Gizmo and the one downstairs to Merlin. Peter diffidently reveals to me that Gizmo has to be allowed to smell the fish-food, which has to be first shaken up and down in its little cardboard carton before the fish upstairs can be fed and that this procedure must be strictly observed however tight the human time schedule might be. After Gizmo has sanctioned that the food is good and the fish may be fed, he then has to be taken to the tank so that he might watch the feeding from its beginning until the last morsel can be seen no more. I am so awestruck at this snippet of intelligence and its being an unwavering rite of passage that I forget to ask Dave if Merlin gets the same treatment down-stairs, but rather assume not on the grounds of horses for courses, or rather cats for fish tanks. Dave, later on in the evening, makes an astute observation of their boys, which on reflection is something I have often unconsciously seen in my three resident cats.

'Have you noticed that when one of them starts to lick himself, the other one immediately seems to go, "Oh yes, good idea, I think I'll have a bit of a lick and polish too"?' The act of imitation is endemic to companion and especially sibling cats it would seem. Dave later embarks on his concerns about Gizmo's recurring attacks on Merlin, almost always that way round, which will start with passionate allogrooming[2] and quickly descend into a full throatal attack on Merlin.

'I shout at him to stop it immediately, I really yell at him. He always pauses and looks up at me with an expression of "don't know why you're shouting at me, I'm not doing anything, really I'm not" and stops and turns away and then the second he thinks I'm no longer watching he just goes straight back into attack mode, straight for poor Merlin's jugular.'

As I drive home I relive the pleasure of a splendid evening spent in the happy exchanges of cat lore, the imbibing of a very decent bottle of dry Chardonnay, the company of two charming men and two magnificent boy cats. Peter and David are waiting to move house and have gone through all the agonies that Michael and I did when looking for the house in Hutton Roof, which is the name of the village we now live in. What will be cat-

---

[2] Allogrooming is the grooming of each other to mutual advantage.

friendly, what will be cat-safe? I greatly look forward to their next chapter.

On 17 November a tiny six-line piece appears in the *Evening Standard* Homes-Gossip page about the cottage, but there is no accompanying photograph as they have run out of space. The description is so low key that I realise reading it that it would be a miracle if any potential buyer responded and, predictably, no buyer does. Michael and I sink into gloom, although we knew that once October had passed the possibility of selling before the end of the year would become ever more elusive, but we are unable to rent it either, and life in the Coach House noticeably tenses up.

CHAPTER 3

I find myself worrying about Fannie and her 'condition', and although I watch her carefully it is hard to tell what her state of mind is. Spasmodically she will suddenly call out, as if she is still on heat, but certainly not for any length of time, nor with the raucous, distracted-but-somehow-driven intensity of her earlier calls. Yesterday she was lying on the sofa next to Titus – the only source of heat in the Coach House at this time being from the wood-burning stove – when I witnessed a new piece of behaviour. She started to groom Titus, which she often does, but as she started the process it became noticeably more intense than her normal spit and polish. She did a thorough going over of both eyes – corners, lids, lashes – and then started a most earnest excavation within Titus's ears, pushing her tongue right down inside them, at which point Titus started to object. Fannie immediately clamped her front leg over Titus and pinioned her to the sofa, so that she was unable to move. Titus dropped her ears down unhappily into the Yoda position, but surprisingly sat still and let it happen to her. Fannie had a completely mesmerised expression on her face, as if she were barely aware of what she was doing and I felt most strongly that I was witnessing a rehearsal on autopilot of things that she will need to do in the future. She continues to look for new places to climb into and is constantly hiding inside the spare room wardrobe. On the other hand her weight does not seem to have changed very much. It might have increased slightly but it is hard to be sure. I should weigh her, of course, but already it is too late for that.

Today is Saturday and I hear our ship's bell outside the door clanging loudly and, as I run downstairs, I can see our village friends, Jeff and

Karen, with their two daughters, Lesley and Alex, smiling in a group outside.

'We've come to look at Fannie,' Alex beams up at me.

'Well, come in and have a good look. She will let you hold her.' As I push Fannie forward towards Alex and she gently strokes her, she looks up at me.

'Can we definitely have one of her kittens, please?' she asks me beguilingly. She knows that I have already said they should have one since their lovely cat Tinkerbell died only a few weeks ago. I watch Alex longingly stroking Fannie, and her yearning for animals and gentleness with them reminds me of how passionately I cared for animals at her age too. Some people never grow out of it!

'Alex, you may have first choice. Oh, well, I have promised a female kitten to Peter Warner, the illustrator of the books, but as long as he can have a female you can choose which one you want. I have also said that Janice, my agent, can have one too if there are enough to go round, but I do want one for Fannie to keep as well, but yes, Alex, you shall have one, I promise.' When Alex smiles it is like the sun coming out.

It is now the Sunday preceding the Monday morning of the operation to neuter Titus and Pushkin and with its dawning comes an overwhelming sense of guilt on my part. In the past we have all lived out our lives, the cats and me, without my invasive interference and now I am interfering every which way in their lives. First I consciously take Fannie to a stud – however, in my defence I have waited five years before doing it and this is the very last chance she has of mating and she was calling this last time fit to break my heart – but nevertheless it was my decision not hers and now I am taking Titus and Pushkin to be neutered, again my resolution. And yet, is that true? The truth is that my interference has been there all their lives. I have consciously contained them within the garden, for example, rather than giving them complete freedom as I have deemed it safer for them. I have kept up their inoculations for their own protection. I have allowed Titus to be operated on, twice, most painfully, for her greater good even though through the period of recovery it undoubtedly felt to her for her greater suffering, so to take these decisions now is no more than I have done throughout their lives. And yet, and yet . . .

In some ways my guilt is made worse by the fact that tonight Titus and Pushkin must starve, while it is essential that Fannie eats at regular intervals throughout the night. Because of the open-plan nature of the Coach House I decide that I should sleep in the spare room, which does have a door that can be closed, and have Fannie shut in there with me with her high-protein cat food, leaving the two other cats free to roam in a house with no accessible cat food. As luck would have it I too have to starve, as I am due for a cholesterol test first thing just before I take Tites and Pushie down for their two ops; the difference being, of course, that I know why I am starving and so it makes sense to me, whereas they don't and are really upset about it. Titus in particular sits squarely in front of me and looks up at me with very serious, very large eyes and makes her strangulated squawky miaow more and more demandingly. Eventually Michael and I say strangely formal goodnights to each other and he goes off to his wing and I to mine. I take Fannie into the room with me and after a lot of tossing and turning I get to sleep. At 2.30 a.m. I am woken by a snuffling, scuffling noise outside the door, which is then greeted by an equally noisy set of sniffings my side of the door. I turn the light on and see that Fannie is trying to dig her way out to meet the other two and, of course, when I open the door there is a reception committee made up of one ginger and one grey[3] cat, both of whom manage mysteriously to exude an air on the one hand of feeling betrayed and on the other of being really hungry. What will not have helped the cause is that Fannie will certainly smell of the food that she has been eating through the night, even if she has not communicated the fact to them. I quickly grab the food that was down for her and shove it into a drawer. Fannie is not happy at being separated from them so I decide to leave the food hidden and the door open. For the remainder of the night I get up at hourly intervals and shut Fannie in by herself to allow her to feed and then

---

[3] technically speaking red and blue!

open up again. By 7 a.m. I am actually pleased that this night is over and the dreaded day has begun. It is a strange fact but, yet again, once I have actually left them in the tender hands of the vet nurse Liz, having waved cheerfully across the lobby at Gerard and then rather embarrassingly nearly bursting into tears while I ask Liz in a wobbly voice to be sure to phone me as soon as she has news, I feel absurdly cheerful. I have renounced my responsibility. I no longer have any decision left to take. It is out of my hands and what will be, will be. At 12.30 the gentle Gerard phones me to say that they have come round and they are fine, but he would like to see me about Titus when I come down to collect them. I go down and he tells me that Titus had possibly the largest uterus of any cat he has ever operated on and that the likelihood of her becoming pregnant with so much build-up in it was remote and that it really did need to be removed. His biggest concern is, however, that he thinks she is experiencing pain in her back legs from her earlier operations – a pain akin to arthritis – and he suggests that I put her back on Metacam which she had been on when she last had her patellar operated on. I have to take her back again in a couple of days' time anyway. I take my wounded burdens home and now dread the effect it will have on Fannie. I let them out and they both move quickly towards the feeding station. Titus sits down and starts to eat. Pushkin falls over, picks himself up, and tries to run upstairs but falls over again and then runs away and hunches himself up in a corner. Fannie comes down and sees them both and hisses mildly. Every time she smells the antiseptic on Titus she hisses again, but her hissing is quiet and seems almost involuntary and she clearly recognises Titus as her sister. Cats are so bad to other cats when they return home with vet smells on them. Later on I find Pushkin dragging his bottom across the carpet leaving small streaks of blood behind him. Poor little castrato, what have I done? Titus takes herself up to our bathroom instead of lying with Fannie on the chair in my study, which is where she would normally lie. Later on Pushkin swells up so badly that the following day I take him back to the vet. Liz the vet nurse is wonderfully reassuring and gets another vet, Ben, to come and inject him with antibiotics and give him painkillers. Meanwhile Titus receives an all clear on her condition; she is one brave girl as always, but I am anxious to get her Metacam painkillers into her when we get home.

One weekend Karen and Alex pop in while they are walking so that Alex can stroke Fannie and check up on her unborn kittens. During their visit Alex tells me that Lesley has managed to acquire a young kitten from a pet shop in Manchester who is called Joey and he is currently at home with them. Will I come down and look at him? As ever, with my weakness for kittens, I bound off to meet young Joey. He has darling white socks, a white chest and prominent tabby stripes. When Peter Warner saw him much later he loved his looks and called him a 'classic tabby'. He is so tiny and I reckon that he was no more than six weeks old, if that, when Lesley first saw him. It always dis- tresses me when pet shops sell kittens as they often sell them dangerously under- age, and they need that

time with their mother. Lesley adores him, as does the whole family, but she is having problems with his feeding. He is flea ridden and he needs worming. Each night when they put him to bed in his basket they lie him near a warm hot-water bottle because he is so shivery and cold. Lesley says to me:

'Well, he cost £70 and then we've spent nearly that again in vet's fees.'

'That's awful for you and I'm so sorry but at least he has come to a good home, so it could be worse and he is a safe boy now.'

'We did try cat shelters but they didn't have any kittens, this isn't a good time of year. And then when we saw him in the shop he was the last remaining kitten.'

He doesn't seem to be drinking and I remember Susan Hill, whose cat Tallulah was the grandmother of Fannie and Titus, saying to me that kittens that were in need of cat milk would often benefit from doses of carnation milk, so I suggest that they try that, and it seems to get Joey through this initial problem.

CHAPTER 4

In spite of the anxiety we both feel because of the
lack of the sale of Moon Cottage I find myself
beginning to look forward to our first Christmas
in Hutton Roof. Money is a bit tight, but if you
are able to stay warm and there is enough to eat
and on top of that you look out over 'paradise'
and you are surrounded by animals that hold your
heart and you have the love of a good man or
woman, then life is not all bad. On the good man
or woman front, Michael and I are snapping at
each other from time to time, sometimes quite
fiercely, but we both know that this is a direct
result of our financial situation, which cannot go

on forever and things will surely get better. Just before Christmas a piece about Moon Cottage appears in *Country Living Magazine* and we get very excited. We then receive two calls, which come to nothing. Two days later, we are phoned by our agent who thinks they have found a renter, but they are still awaiting confirmation. This will give us some leeway if it comes off and psychologically it will help.

One day, in a splendid and I might say successful endeavour to cheer me up, my chum Jane tells me on the phone that her late mother had been very fond of a dear farmer in Suffolk who, some time during the sixties, had been the proud guardian of three cats who were fabulously named Magnificat, Terrificat and Gloria-in-excelsis-Deo. I would love to feel that their feline namesakes might walk the land again. While on the subject of Gloria in excelsis Deo, around this time Michael volunteers to join the Christmas carollers on their rounds and on a cold dark evening shortly thereafter he is summoned to a rendezvous in the village, where he meets up with a group of twenty or so grown-ups and children. Hours later he returns, full of good cheer and mince pies and tales of mock horror at the way people have 'paid us off'.

'What do you mean, people paid you off?'

'Well, if anyone had given us a tenner, say, before we actually set out, all the carollers took that as a sign that they would rather we didn't call on them, so although we walked the full length of the village street, at certain houses someone would say, "No, not that one, we've been paid off", etc., but it made it easier because we still stopped at about fifteen houses and we would never have got round them all, so it was a good thing.'

'Did you get invited in by anyone?'

'Oh yes, the Armisteads invited us into their kitchen at the big farm in the village and also Bernard did down at Gale Triangle. He offered us mince pies and wine. That was our last port of call, but if we had started there we would never have got round.' He smiles seraphically. 'It was really nice,' he murmurs happily.

Shortly after the house-to-house carols there is the annual Carol Service accompanied by the Kirkby Lonsdale Brass Band at our little church of St John's, immediately next to the Coach House, and although I have been to many carol services in my life this one is simply the most lovely, for its simplicity and the feeling of love and warmth that seems to radiate from everyone there. The church is lit up enchantingly and looks quite beautiful with its splendid decorations of flowers and holly and ivy and it is packed. As we stand jammed into our little pew singing 'God Rest Ye Merry Gentlemen, Let Nothing Ye Dismay', I am overwhelmed with a sense of everlastingness.

Johnny and Oliver, Michael's two youngest sons, both come up for Christmas and the celebrations start in earnest. On Christmas Day, to my childish delight, when I first look out of the window I find the entire world outside has turned white.

'Michael, wake up! Look! Look! We really do have a white Christmas!'

'Don't believe you,' he mumbles from under the warm duvet.

'Go on, go on, get up and see it!' I wallop him with a pillow. But as he lifts himself up on one elbow that wonderful eerie bluey-white can be seen round the edges of the pale cream curtains. He rushes to the window and flings the curtains apart.

'Wayhay, that's FANTASTIC!'

I run downstairs and let the cats out. As always when they tread in snow they fastidiously shake each paw as if that will sort it out once and for all and then put their feet down again and stop and shake again, perplexed at this cold white stuff. They peer nervously through the fence into the field at the back, but because it is totally unrecognisable to them, they stay in the garden and eventually all three of them sit in a line on the bench looking around them. Soon they quietly jump down and come back inside the house.

Later on in the day, just before the sun drops below the horizon, I go out for a solitary walk and climb part of the way up the crag behind us so I can look down over the village. Seeing the little houses huddled together with their bright lights twinkling out and the smoke floating up from many a chimney is strangely affecting. Being not part of it and yet part of it is sad and beautiful at the same time. Being on the outside looking in through the windows, being a small element within this village and being made so welcome and yet knowing we may still have the entire dream snatched away is heart-rending. I sit down on a small outcrop of rock and watch the light over the Yorkshire fells until the sun starts to sink behind me. As the sun starts to set, the monochrome world in front of me changes from its stark varying shades of white broken only by the brown bracken twigs sticking up through the snow, to a glorious pink and then burgundy red as the reflection of the sun bleeds across the snow and over the ice-covered summit of Ingleborough in one majestic farewell to daylight and the end of Christmas Day.

The snow stays for another couple of days and

then almost imperceptibly melts away and our green, brown and purple landscape is restored to us in its former glory.

Several days have passed since Christmas and Fannie has been sick again, this morning, twice. She has had this intermittent sickness for a couple of weeks and it does seem to be very like a feline form of morning sickness. She keeps miaowing, but I'm not sure what she wants nor, I think, is she. Pushkin is much better and now at last walking with his tail up. Titus, on the other hand, although she showed little side-effect of the hysterectomy at the beginning and is self-evidently stoic, is obviously in quite a lot of pain still and currently hates to be picked up by either of us. She is such a sweet-natured cat and so forgiving.

January is upon us and so far there has been a worrying silence from our agent, but finally on the third of January we are told at last that our renter will be taking possession of the cottage on the seventh. We celebrate this event in a low-key manner, but it is a great deal better than not having a renter.

It is now seven weeks since Fannie was mated by

Zimmy with just over two weeks to go if she is indeed pregnant. 'If' must seem a slightly surprising thing to say at this stage, but although her uterus is undoubtedly swollen, there hasn't been any noticeable change in her size for the last couple of weeks. I am fearful that the litter might be very small or, worse, that the growth of the kittens has stopped altogether. Since Pushkin has been neutered and recovered, he is far more energetic than he used to be and chases both of the girls at least twice daily, quite vigorously. Fannie always hisses at him; Titus more often than not just claims 'pax' by lying on a bed somewhere to keep out of the firing line. I am feeding Fannie more highly concentrated kitten food and Pushkin is eating it too, could this be the reason? When he gets close to them he merely wants to pounce at them not mount them, but they both appear to dislike it from their responses.

Tuesday night and we have gales that it later transpires do untold damage to the whole county. For the first time since we moved into Cumbria I am really frightened. I lie in our huge bed and listen to the wind howling. We have three windows in our bedroom, one facing north, one east and one west, and as I lie there the wind buffeting every surface of the house begins to sound like hugely amplified wild beasts, chomping, whining, squeaking, and squalling around the house. I keep hearing distant bangings of doors and rattling of windows in the other part of the house and sometimes in a brief lull I just catch the rustle of one or other of the cats moving around restlessly. Michael, bless him, doesn't hear a sound because he has been working his socks off all week down at Moon Cottage, getting it ready for the renter, and arrives back in the early evening, exhausted and falls into a deep coma-like sleep. Trouble is when you are lying next to someone who is fast asleep and you are frightened, it is strangely lonelier than if you are alone when you can get up and make a cup of tea and turn the lights on. I am aware of his brother, John, too, who is on the other side of the house and I know he is a light sleeper, so I imagine he is sleeping only fitfully if at all with this fearsome racket. In between the huge sounds of the roaring wind the rain lashes at the house in a way I have never heard it before and now a new worry starts.

Will the wind get under the tiles and lift the whole roof off? The wind does seem to be alive almost; it pauses as if in some way it is mustering its energy and then it comes in and hits the house apparently on three sides with a massive sound and then it goes quiet again and then another huge onslaught. This is wind at its most savagely brutal.

In the morning we go out nervously to see what the damage is. We find branches, huge branches, the size of small trees, ripped off our Scots Pines, fallen in the road outside. A farmer with the aid of his tractor has moved one of the branches which was blocking the road to the side so we now cannot get our cars out of our little yard, but we just feel such relief that they appear not to have damaged any passers-by, which they so easily might have done. We are without electricity for twenty-four hours, but I quite enjoy the challenge of cooking on top of the wood-burning stove. Not having hot water is less amusing, however. There are terrible floods in Carlisle and we realise, bad though it has been, we got off lightly compared with other parts of Cumbria. Five nights later we have more of the same. The noise from the woodland behind the

house is particularly spooky, with repeated creak-
ing and crashing sounds, and indeed afterwards we
find there are many ancient trees which have been
uprooted and much forest is laid low. On this
second night of high winds the cats patrol the
house more restlessly than the first night and are
clearly very alarmed. I wonder too on such nights
how high the mortality of birds, small mammals
and insects might have been.

CHAPTER 5

Following the great gales I receive a phone call from Hilary, our friend in the village, who has two cats, Thomas, her long-term resident neutered tom, and Ollie, a three-quarters-grown male kitten who appeared on Halloween in need of a home. Hilary adores Ollie, who is jet-black and shiny like a little olive, hence his name, although they have had problems with him from early on. He started to wet their bed. Hilary reckons it was because he was frightened of Thomas but also because he was just entering his difficult 'teens'. She took Ollie to be neutered just before Christmas and that seemed to have resolved the problem.

Now, however, she sounds at the end of her tether. He has started 'performing' in the dining-room, downstairs, close to the window, behind the curtains, and this time it is bowels as well as bladder that he is evacuating. I can tell that if the problem is not resolved soon she is going to be forced to rehome Ollie, and she clearly doesn't want to do this. I feel slightly helpless as I would offer to take him for her, but I cannot with Fannie's brood about to be born. I take her down a copy of a brilliant book by Celia Haddon, the pet correspondent for the *Daily Telegraph*, called *Chats with Cats: How to Read Your Cat's Mind*,[4] in which, among other feline problems, she very sensitively discusses the stress factors that might make cats go to the toilet outside their litter trays and how to resolve the impasse. Having read that chapter again I suggest to Hilary that it might be other cats trying to get in through their cat flap, or through the French windows, or even the stress of the gales that is upsetting poor little Ollie, as my own cats were

---

[4] *Chats with Cats: How to Read Your Cat's Mind* by Celia Haddon (Little Books Ltd., 2004) £8.99 ISBN 19044 3531 9.

clearly very disturbed by them. Hilary agrees to read the book and see if they can work out a modus vivendi. I make a promise to her, however, that if it doesn't work out I will find Ollie a home.

Today I go down to the vet's to pick up some kitten food for Fannie and see Gerard just as he is about to start operating. I shout out gaily:

'Hope I won't have to call you out on the night of the twenty-second or twenty-third, but are you around? Those are the nights that Fannie should perform.' He groans back at me in mock alarm. Earlier on when I had taken Titus and Pushkin back for their post-op check-ups I had told Gerard how worried I was about Fannie being small, but he had said if it is a small litter, cats often don't show very much beforehand. It could just be a couple of kittens.

Fannie continues to search assiduously throughout each day for a nesting place, and I am having ongoing problems with Pushkin wanting to be in every possible litterbed I provide and Fannie not liking to lie in it after Pushkin's smell is there. She continually grooms Titus vigorously in an instinctive rehearsal for what is to come and Titus is clearly not terribly amused by the unrelenting ablutions she is forced to endure.

Today is the sixty-third day from the first mating of Zimmy and Fannie, and Marje, the breeder and carer of Zimmy who phones up from time to time to check how things are going, says that if Fannie makes it until the sixty-fourth day, tomorrow in other words, there should be no problem with the survival of the kittens. Fannie seems in very good health. She is full of beans and she is eating like a horse. She is slightly more jumpy than usual, but I am sure that is normal as her instinct must be telling her she is vulnerable.

Michael and I are now sleeping in the spare bedroom as it is more likely that this is where Fannie will choose to have her kittens and from now on it could be any time, and my most experienced kitten-midwives seem to think early hours of the morning is optimum time usually. We rose this morning early, by our new standard of living that is to say, at 6.30 as Michael is going to the christening of his grand-nephew, but I am staying on kitten watch back at home and there is a breathtaking sunrise which has taken several glorious hours. There was an iron-hard frost overnight and the eastern sky in front of us is ablaze with a huge red globe of a sun and the day is promising to be gorgeous.

Later on, Karen, Alex and Lesley all come up, as they have most weekends, to see how Fannie is progressing and Alex, who is yearning for one of the kittens, strokes her gently. Alex is also scrupulous and wants to say hullo to Titus who has stayed out of the way asleep, so just before they leave I take her up to my study where we find Titus and she makes a big fuss of her. Alex is a born cat lover. Lesley's young kitten, Joey, is now doing very well and is spending more time at Hutton Roof to Alex's delight. Alex loves Joey because he will play with her, although she tells me he bites her playfully, but she missed this with Tinks a bit because 'he was always Daddy's cat, and that was it!'

Another day comes and goes and Fannie's sixty-fifth day of pregnancy dawns, which one of the feline websites says is the true average length of time for most domestic cats.

She is currently nesting in the box down to the

right of my desk which is where I would love her to have them, and certainly where I would love her to nurse them, so I can keep an eye on them and the other cats too, but yesterday Titus kept sitting in there and simply wouldn't get out. Titus has left it alone so far today, but just now as I was writing this, when she tried to join Fannie in the box, Fannie very gently pushed her away, so now she is lying in front of Fannie half in and half out of it.

One of the things that made me laugh this morning is that Titus, who again insisted on sharing the box with Fannie, had her bottom very thoroughly cleaned and looked completely outraged while it was happening and eventually struck out mildly at Fannie, but clearly Fannie's instinct to 'mother' is so strong that she was unable to resist it. So at the end of that round, Titus stays put in the box and Fannie gets out and goes into the cold bedroom. But right now she has come back and is lying on my lap, purring loudly.

This morning, on the sixty-sixth day, Fannie is more urgently than before searching for a nesting place, so surely it must be closer now. Marje last night on the phone urged me to phone the vet 'by tomorrow morning' if nothing has happened. One of the things that is strange is that Titus seems to have taken on the symptoms of pregnancy along with Fannie. She is lying in the box and seems strange in the same way that Fannie is.

I am trying like mad not to get stressed out, but it is very tense-making, this waiting and not knowing what is going to happen. I have a gut feeling that it is going to be tomorrow now, but I am beginning to be really concerned.

The following day we find Titus repeatedly licking Fannie, who is cowering down allowing it to happen, looking very subdued, which is the complete reverse of Fannie's previously zealous administrations to Titus. It is as if Titus is comforting her in some way. I phone the vet's and tell them that Fannie is now overdue and I am worried and I need them to take a look at her. I take her down and Gerard agrees to scan her. He shaves her belly and puts a large animal scanner on her because his small animal scanner is not around. As I watch his face my heart sinks.

'There are no kittens in here, I am fairly certain, unless she has two tiny ones hidden up under her ribcage. Are you sure she couldn't have had some kittens and they are lying dead somewhere? Her nipples are engorged and she has all the appearance of a pregnant cat, but her belly isn't large enough for a litter I would say, so she must have lost them.'

I know there are no dead kittens and I explain to him that I have been sleeping with her every night for the last four nights with the door shut and there is nowhere she could have hidden them. He looks mystified.

I put Fannie back in the carrying cage and by the time I get her home her stomach has shrunk and there is no appearance of pregnancy of any kind. In deference to Gerard I look all round the spare bedroom for any dead kittens, but there are none as I had assumed. I get on to the internet and look up 'feline phantom pregnancy' and very quickly I realise that poor little Fannie has gone through the full term of an imagined pregnancy right up to producing milk. Cats have phantom pregnancies more rarely than dogs because they are induced ovulators so must have been mated in order to go through it, and the chances then are that they will have been impregnated, whereas with dogs a hormonal bitch could just believe she is pregnant without being anywhere near a dog. Therefore it is unusual for a vet who doesn't deal regularly with cat breeders (in these days of widespread spayed cats from an early age) to encounter feline phantom pregnancies whereas canine 'phantoms' are much more common.

Fannie herself is all right but I would say she has the air of a very depressed cat. Could that possibly have been why Titus was first imitating her and then consoling her? She already knew then that it was 'wrong' in some way? Fannie just takes herself off to the chair in my study and Titus lies curled up next to her, and I leave them to work it out with each other. She has now stopped looking in the nesting boxes and so with a heavy heart I remove them all and return the house to its previous order.

Michael and I are both utterly devastated by it and I feel completely flattened and empty. We had wanted kittens from Fannie more than I can easily explain and if this is how we feel, how much worse is it for that poor little cat? I phone Peter and break the bad news to him and he is, of course, disappointed but very understanding, and then that evening I phone Alex. Alex is heart-broken and says:

'Oh, I'll never get a kitten now, it will never happen.' I try to reassure her that somehow I will find a way and she will get a kitten.

CHAPTER 6

By coincidence on 26 January I receive two emails of note, both about Pushkin. The first is from reader Rita Lawson in Durham, who responds to something I have said in one of my books about cats and their powers of reasoning, which I strongly believe I witnessed in Pushkin when he was trying to escape from his enclosure in Moon Cottage and she too has observed how they can solve problems by thinking hard about them.

From: Rita Lawson
To: Marilyn Edwards
Sent: Wednesday, January 26, 5:51 pm
Subject: Sam and his thought processes

Dear Marilyn

I have two cats, Lucy and Sam, and in response to your story about cats thinking through problems, I have one about Sam. If Lucy tries something and it doesn't work, she forgets about it and gets on with something else. She has no patience, but Sam is a different kettle of fish.

He has a 'thing' about plastic bags (I can never leave any lying about, as he gets inside them!). He saw me one day with a plastic bag of sugar, and saw that I had put it in a top kitchen cupboard. No problem, he thought, I can open doors, but what he didn't know was that that door opened from the left side and not the right, so he was trying to open the hinge side.

He sat on the floor and stared up at that cupboard for about 20 minutes, before jumping onto the worktop, onto the extractor fan and from there onto the top of the offending cupboard. He then opened the cupboard with his paw from the top, leaned over, and delicately lifted out the bag of sugar with one claw, dropped it onto the ground and jumped down after it. Success!!!!

And then a little later I receive this addendum from Rita about something that happened to a friend of hers:

My friend told me this story that I thought was just great. If I had read about it in a magazine I would not have believed it, but this was a tale about her own dog and cat.

The animals were not allowed in the bedroom so every night the bedroom door was shut firmly. However, one morning the cat was found on the bed and the dog on the bedroom floor. Margaret told her husband, Roy, off for not shutting the door, but this happened night after night.

The mystery was solved one day when they caught the culprits in the act.

The dog was standing with his nose pressed against the bedroom door, the cat jumped onto the dog's shoulders, then proceeded to reach up and pull down the door handle with his paws and the dog then pressed on the door with his nose and opened it!

I just love it. Hoping all are well, both humans and felines!!

Rita

What is especially wonderful about this second story is that it gives weight to the concept of cross-species communication and then the question is, who thought it out? My money goes on the cat as the solution depended upon one of the animals envisaging the manipulation of the handle, and that had to be the animal that was going to be the highest up.

The second email is from Ruth, who has a cat called Pushkin, and some extraordinary instinct in her makes her ask me where I got my Pushkin. By a process of elimination via email we find that both Pushkins came from the same breeder, Mary White, and are cousins, well at any rate definitely related, and I enclose this extract from her about her Pushkin because it is very typical of a Russian Blue boy. Ruth's Pushkin is about six months younger than my lad.

From: Ruth
To: Marilyn
Sent: Wednesday, January 26, 1:58 AM
Subject: Pushkin and Pushkin!

Dear Marilyn

I have kept in touch with Mary White from time to time and sent her photos of Pushkin. They had a baby a couple of years ago and have given up breeding cats and have had them all spayed, so my Pushkin was one of the last of the line. We don't have any other animals (although I'd like more).

My Pushkin is a cat of deep thoughts and, as you say in your book: if only we could get inside the cat's mind! But I guess that's what makes them so incredibly fascinating. And those disdainful looks: when I'm singing loving songs to him, or speaking in that silly baby-talk way telling him how beautiful he is, or dancing around with him in my arms . . . *what on earth is she doing now? Put me down, I'm far too dignified for this type of behaviour. I'm Russian for goodness sake not a common type of cat!* . . .

He certainly is a one-person cat and, although he's

gone through periods of not wanting to sit on me or be affectionate, he has now settled into spending time snuggling up to me, on the bed or chair and I just love it. Of course, one can't possibly move until he decides to jump off or my arm goes dead, whichever comes soonest. He also loves to head-butt everything, but he has never done that rubbing around the legs that other cats so often do. His most endearing thing is to snuggle right up in my arms and rub the back of his head hard against my face. Also, he makes lots of funny grunts and groans while he is sleeping; sometimes I do them back and can have quite a grunty/groany conversation with him!

Kindest wishes,

Ruth

In the Coach House, cat life resumes a normality of sorts. Fannie continues to be depressed, but slowly she recovers and her nipples very quickly shrink back to normal. Gerard thought she had actually lactated they were so swollen, but the very acts of taking her in the car to the vet and the trauma of shaving her for the scan seem to have speeded up the 'termination' of the imagined pregnancy, and since then I have spoken to two other cat breeders who have experienced the same sort of scenario. I ask various experts whether they think I should risk taking Fannie to the stud again, but the consensus is that as a near-maiden cat of six years of age I would be exposing her to unnecessary risks by pursuing the possibility of her breeding again. Within days she is back on heat again and with this her spirits lift and ours sink, as she is astoundingly vocal. However, I am glad that she is feeling so much better. Nature is a remarkable healer as well as trickster.

Michael and I agonise about what we should do. We had always intended to have one litter from the kittens that grew up to be Fannie and Titus, and that was why Pushkin joined our household. Having lived all this time in the belief that Fannie was going to have kittens we feel bereft now by their absence. We talk about future possibilities and throw various ideas up in the air. After a while I ponder, as with everything in life, has it happened for a purpose? I assume from her silence that Hilary is still worrying about Ollie, and so I decide I should take this as a sign and I write her a letter.

This is an extract from it:

The Coach House – 9 February

Dear Hilary,
Am writing you a little letter rather than
ringing you . . . to give you a chance to think
this through before you phone me.

Michael and I have talked Ollie over and
have decided to offer him a home with us
with our cats, but it is of course risky
because of Pushkin and if it turns out that
Ollie still has his incontinence problems we
would have to find an alternative home for
him, but because Pushkin is very gentle it is
just possible it will work out OK between
them. (I am envisaging trouble between the
males as that is how it usually is, but of
course the females could be a problem too!)

However, it is just possible that in the
meantime you have found a way of all living
together and you would rather he stayed with
you, hence the letter, because I want you to
be sure either way.

I have been advised not to let Fannie get pregnant and what I would ideally like to do, therefore, is get a young female kitten and breed from her, and if we take Ollie on then I couldn't do that, because I will simply have too many cats . . . Having said all that, I would love to give him a home and would do everything within my power to make it work out for him.

Hilary . . . could you phone me when you have had a chance to digest all this and let me know how you feel and if you want him to go, when I can come and collect him?

All the best,

Marilyn and Michael

This produces a phone call by return from Hilary, who very positively tells me that things have improved completely at their house and that Ollie and Thomas are getting on fine and Ollie has stopped soiling the dining-room – she has been using the Feliway plug-in pheromone and that has helped, but whatever was stressing him has ceased. The whole family have discussed Ollie and his future and are appalled at the idea that I might take him away and that it is very sweet of me to offer, but they definitely do not want Ollie to leave them. I am absolutely delighted for them and also I find relieved for me too, as I so want to pursue the idea of acquiring a female kitten, and this now frees me up to do that.

Ann, a book-selling friend from the West Country, comes to us en route for a family holiday. Ann, quietly spoken, gentle and cat mad, enters the house and refuses to be coerced upstairs to her room where I want to make her feel at home, but insists instead on pursuing a long schmoozey introduction of herself to all three of the cats. Even the one-person-loving Pushkin, Mr-Timid-Incarnate, responds briefly to her overtures before wandering off to find a suitable spot for a nice sleep. Fannie spends some considerable time taking her on board, watching her and then lying near her, squinting sneakily at her through half-closed eyes while pretending to be asleep (in fact she does this for the whole of Ann's visit). But Titus – now there – I have never seen anything like it. Immediately, there is an exceptional rapport between them. To begin with Titus just lies down and over on her back for her tummy to be rubbed, as she does with anyone and everyone who is prepared to invest their time in this way – such a floozy – but soon it develops beyond that. Having been doing chores out in the kitchen, I return to the sitting-room to find Titus sitting upright on Ann's knee, her eyes half closed in a semi-transcendental state, her head held high and her white bib to the fore, with an expression of such supreme self-satisfaction on her face that it defies belief. She maintains this expression of extreme rapture for what seems to me like hours and I have to say I'm pretty impressed with Ann's endurance too. Later on I overhear Ann whispering to Titus about a little visit to

Gloucester and Titus looks back up at her with large quiescent eyes. As Pushkin saunters across the dining-room table for a brief head-butt and Ann runs her hand along his muscled flank admiringly, I explain how frustrating it was that he never attempted to mate with either Fannie or Titus and there always seemed to have been some block there of some kind. Ann laughs and says:

'Oh, I do know what you mean. It's like when you see a really attractive man and then you discover he's gay and as a woman you just can't help feeling "what a waste!"'

I discover that Ann, who has had many cats in her life, when searching for a new companion cat who in the event became her beloved Bella, went to a cat sanctuary in Stafford where she then lived. As soon as she arrived a beautiful black cat came towards her and when she put her hand out to it, the cat climbed straight up her shoulder and wrapped itself around her. She turns to me as she is telling me this and smiles disarmingly:

'Oh, I just knew that that cat would do that to everyone and anyone; I was sure that the very next person who came in would get that treatment and find it a home. But when I saw the tortoiseshell cat that is Bella she was scrunched up in the back of the cage with body language saying, "Don't touch me – don't come near me – leave me alone" and I knew it was her that I needed to take home with me.'

Ann, having got Bella home with the full assurance from the sanctuary that the young couple who had brought the cat into them for rehoming because they had started their own human family and did not feel a cat could be kept in a household with a new baby (on which subject Ann's comment, which I share, is "rubbish") had had the cat injected and spayed, was somewhat disconcerted when Bella started to show all the signs of being on heat. She was so much in denial of this as the possible explanation of Bella's miaowings and rollings around that she looked up all manner of diseases in the belief that it might be something else that was ailing her young queen. She finally took her to her local vet who assured her that Bella was indeed on heat and offered to do the operation the next day, which he duly did.

On the day that Ann prepares to take her leave of

us all I find myself actively counting feline heads, as it hasn't gone without my notice that she is the owner of a large, squashy sort of zip-up canvas holdall that could be quite useful for cat-carrying purposes. But in the end, after she has gone there are still three cats, all present and correct, so it was all talk, Titus, all talk!

CHAPTER 7

Michael and I have several conversations about how we should go about tracking down a kitten, but he is seriously distracted by the lodger in Moon Cottage, who keeps making complaint after complaint about equipment not working and other problems, and both he and the agent are beginning to be exasperated by it.

I try a local cat rescue home but there are no kittens needing homes, only spayed cats, so I try local farmers but again nothing doing. I have been studying different breeds and am attracted to the Bengal cat for two reasons: they are very beautiful, of course, but also and more importantly they have very outgoing personalities and, while I adore Pushkin, his tendency to imitate the dormouse and keep himself strictly to himself can be slightly maddening. My friend Sue always teases me, as the guardian of Siamese and Devon Rex all noted for their outspoken behaviour, with phrases like: 'Come on, Marilyn, when are you going to get a real cat?' Actually I am not sure that she has ever actually said that, but I know that is what she thinks. In fact, Sue is due to visit us in the near future, so I decide I must get the ball rolling on the kitten-acquiring front, pronto. I start to put out feelers with different breeders and finally discover that melanistic (black) Bengal cats[5] are considered less desirable to anyone who is breeding Bengal cats since their colour is not accepted by the Bengal Cat Club as suitable and as a result they are sold as pets for markedly less than the asking price of the standard Bengal.[6] There are two types of patterns

---

[5] The Black Bengal, or melanistic Bengal occurs occasionally in Bengal litters. Both parents must carry the recessive gene in order for a melanistic Bengal to appear in a litter.

[6] The asking price for a standard Bengal queen to be used for breeding is considerably higher than most other breeds of cat.

in Bengals: the Spotted (Leopard) and the Marble, and many variations of colour within these patterns, but black is shunned as a breeding colour. I am astonished. Black cats are just beautiful creatures, almost always they have astonishingly shiny fur and vivid green or amber eyes; it is so strange to me that they are ostracised in this way.

Here is a wonderful poem, sent to me by Doreen Dann, which she wrote from her own experience in the cat sanctuary where she works, and it made my heart ache:

The Kitten House or Why not a Black One?

'Oh, see that pretty one fluffy and sweet,
Little white legs and four tiny grey feet'
Please look at the dark shape alone at the back,
I'm cuddly, I'm pretty, but I'm also BLACK.

'Come see the tabbies with markings so fine,
Look at that ginger one, Oh let it be mine'
We are the dark shapes – there at the back,
We're cute and adorable but, sadly, we're BLACK

If you want a pet that will love you to bits,
Come, take a look at these little BLACK kits.
Our eyes will shine just as bright as those others,
Just give us a cuddle – me, and my brothers!

Look into my eyes, what do you see?
A beautiful kitten, so playful – that's me.
You've seen all the pretty ones – now choose from
   the back,
Say 'look at that treasure, it's mine – and it's
BLACK'.

© Doreen Dann 2000

Two different breeders I approach have black
Bengal female kittens for sale and both agree to
allow me to breed one litter on three conditions.
The first condition is that I must have the cat
spayed after one litter; the second condition is that
any kittens from that litter may not be allowed to
breed; and the third condition I volunteer, which is
that I won't sell any of the kittens from the one
litter I am allowed to have, but give them away only
to friends whom I trust to adhere to this
agreement. In the end I decide to pursue the

northernmost breeder as the kitten is older and therefore likely to be ready to have kittens that much sooner, added to which I like the way they look after their cats and the way they sound. They live in a large house and the cats are free to roam around the house and it has none of the feel of a kitten factory that some cat breeders exude. So, having researched this far and, of course, after long conversations with Michael, I pick up the phone and commit!

At this point Sue comes to stay with me and teases me about my condition of 'pregnant' anticipation at the delights of the black ball of bliss that is about to enter my life. I love Sue's company and she is wise beyond words on the manners and motivations of cats, not to mention Victorian prints, counter-tenors, music in general, organic gardening, cookery, books, reading and all other manner of things. She has, however, just reached a difficult stage with her companions of many years as her cat Chatto, sister to her existing cat Johnnie, has recently died leaving her with one twenty-year-old Siamese cat, Johnnie, whom she hand-reared with a tiny bottle when she was just a wee sick scrap of a kitten and two young and energetic Devon Rexes, so we have much cat talk to catch up on.

After Sue departs, I set off on my great expedition North, where I find the house and meet the Bengal breeders, a gentle young couple who care a lot about their cats, and I am introduced to their black girl, whom they call Beauty. She sashays into the room and I am enchanted by her sleek shiny black looks and her striking gold-green eyes. She is the essence of feline femininity and from her first entrance she dramatically grabs the attention of all who watch her. This one demands centre stage. She starts a completely manic game with the man of the house who is holding out a rod with an elastic string and a feather at its end, and she jumps high and repeatedly like a true jack-in-the-box. I am next introduced to her mother, who is an elegant tawny-coloured spotted Bengal with well-defined rosettes and she is very striking; she looks exactly like a miniature leopard. They play-fight amiably with each other on the carpet in front of the fire and I feel an enormous pang of guilt at knowing that I am about to take this lively kitten away from her mother. At more than seventeen weeks she is old to be with her mother still and she has been fully weaned for some weeks, so the older cat is probably more than ready to see her go. She was born near the end of October, which makes her a Halloween kitten I suddenly realise with pleasure. I ask if I may hold her, and they warn me, laughingly, that although she has been well socialised, she is still outspoken about when and how she will be handled. As I scoop her up she makes a deep, loud, almost boorish protest, but as I turn her on her back and she continues her vocal remonstration, she also starts to purr simultaneously. Her fur is the softest, silkiest fur I have ever touched. I am new to the world of the Bengal, but now I understand their allure. Her eyes hold mine unblinkingly. They have a determined look in them, but also they are full of emotion. I find myself extraordinarily moved by her and a little awestruck; she has a beauty to her that is almost that of a wild creature, something akin to the quality of an unbroken horse. She isn't perfect, though; she has strange broken whiskers and the end of her tail is oddly lumpy. I find myself falling madly in love with this black, purring, protesting, noisy, wriggling, bouncy creature. The couple who run this business are very kind and spend a long time initiating me in the things that make Bengals different from other cats and in the problems that I might expect to encounter from early on, and I am touched at how concerned they are about what is to happen to their kittens once they start their new life. Assuring them all will be well, together we bundle her up and put her in the cat carrier and I take my leave.

On the long drive South she protests sporadically, but most especially at the beginning of the journey after which she sleeps. For the rest of the journey from time to time she wakes and squawks for a few minutes and then again falls silent. I try to suppress all thoughts of what her mother may be going through now with a greater knowledge than her offspring of this habit of kitten-kidnap; also of what she herself may be thinking of this unfriendly business of being snatched, boxed and put into a sick-making moving noisy machine or of the grief that the breeders feel at losing their beloved black kitten. To help me expunge these dire thoughts, I sing songs, loudly, and then I go on to tell her all sorts of things, although I fail to mention the big scary cats back at the Coach House and eventually she gets bored and falls asleep.

When we first get back to the Coach House I feel a new pang of guilt as I realise that I may not have appreciated the degree to which the world for the resident cats is likely to change with the introduction of the new kitten. I walk in, swinging the cat carrier and its burden, and watch Titus and Fannie begin their reaction to it. Fannie hisses at a few feet away, Titus just sits back and scents the air. Pushkin emerges after half an hour and is

silently curious and just watches, and then he slinks away to mull it over on his own. Fannie continues to hiss like a steaming kettle on the hob. Michael takes the lid off the carrier and lets out the little black cat, while I stroke the ever agitated Fannie. The kitten is surprisingly brave and immediately does the rounds of the room, apparently completely unabashed by the adjacent hissing. The breeders have given me the igloo on which she always slept and I have it on the floor beside me and from time to time she returns to base, just to check that it is still there. Michael watches her entranced and I see him also falling for her hook, line and sinker. We talk of her name. All the cats in the Coach House are named after writers or characters in books, and although Beauty[7] would fit that category, such terrible things happened to that poor horse that I find myself resistant to it. However, she was born close to Halloween and it was close to Halloween a year earlier that Giles Gordon, writer, poet, agent and dear friend died, so I decide I would like to name

---

[7] as in Black Beauty.

her in his memory. As she is so completely feminine Michael and I agree on 'Gilly', with a hard G as in 'ghillie'[8] – Giles, being a Scot would have liked that – so Gilly it is from now on. As soon as I had got Gilly back to the Coach House I had phoned her former home and reported on her progress and that night I do the promised email update before we turn in for the night:

Things are better now. The three resident cats have all retired to different sleeping places and are leaving her alone. She is currently on her igloo by Michael (who has fallen in love with her totally as I knew he would) and she has eaten quite a lot (of your biscuits, for the moment she won't touch ours but I'm sure that will change) and she has used the cat litter tray once and she has played quite a lot and walked around. She has climbed a tall set of library steps. Climbed into the sink, got behind the dustbin in the kitchen and a couple of times she has let out the most heartbreaking squawks which I am sure are for you both and for her mum and her feline mates,

---

[8] or as in that old song, Gilly, Gilly, Ossenfeffer, Katzenellen Bogen by the Sea.

but tonight will be the worst for her and then it will get better. She is going to be fine I can tell and she can more than hold her own against my bunch of wimps – she is loved already by us both I promise you.

CHAPTER 8

On this first night I feel I need to give her full, exclusive attention, so I opt to sleep alone with her in the spare room, which has a door, and leave Michael to say the ritualistic goodnight to the three adult cats on his bed in solitary splendour. When I first walk into the room and get into bed, little Gilly is utterly miserable and walks around the room wailing, and my heart sinks – poor little mite! I call her several times, and eventually she comes to me and then, as brave as a lion, a rather small lion, she buries herself under the duvet and sleeps stretched out next to me, pretty soundly too. At some point during the night Titus tries to dig her way in under the door, which is shortly followed by Fannie making a loud protesting miaowing outside, but we stick it out à deux until Michael and I both have to leave for church in the morning. I leave Gilly shut in the spare bedroom, which is at least familiar territory and has a cat litter tray and food in it, and when we get back she seems fine and I settle down to work in my study, where she joins me. Titus, as ever, is the one who tries to make friends, but now there is a lot of hiss and spit coming from Gilly back at her. Pushkin, when he comes close to her, doesn't hiss unless he is hissed at and then he hisses back, but she doesn't like him. Sadly, however, it is Fannie who is the big problem for Gilly. And Fannie reciprocates her dislike with equal fervour. Every time the two of them are in a room together there is a lot of noise. Gilly has now consumed copious amounts of food and water, so I feel I can relax in that department at least. It was wonderful that the breeders gave me her igloo. That was such a clever and thoughtful thing to do because it clearly has very important smells of home for little Gilly. As I write this, she is lying on it completely exhausted, in the deepest cat sleep I have ever seen.

Several days have now passed and one of the things that is remarkable about little Gilly since she has been with us is her voracious appetite for real food. I remember now that Pushkin was just like this until he too became addicted to his Hill's biscuits, like the other two. At the moment Gilly is eating the last of the biscuits that the breeder gave me for her although she has flirted a bit with Hill's Rabbit, but it is sardines (with the tomato sauce rinsed off, but not in oil) and pilchards (ditto) and underdone lamb laced with garlic cut up small, but the lamb has to have been freshly cooked not reheated, that send her into a frenzy. She needs only to get a whiff of one of these on offer and she bounds into the kitchen, races up the library steps, walks along the kitchen units (clumsily, her balance is not very good still) and round the edge of the sink and yaps. Her demands are both raucous and rude, and they make me laugh. However, one of the most gorgeous things she does when her nose is well into her bowl of sardines, or whatever it is that she is currently loving, is to emit a muffled series of 'mnnn, yumnnn, yummmn' sounds of sensual bliss, the like of which I have never heard from a cat before. She is almost crying from pleasure.

One of the first of our neighbours to meet Gilly is Richard, from next door, and knowing how he loves to tease me about the cats I am braced for trouble. I am completely unnerved, therefore, when he first sets his eyes on her and says with genuine admiration in his voice:

'Now that's what I call a real cat, that one. I can see she has a *big* personality.' Then later, as he carefully studies her, he adds:

'But I *am* worried that she might be a hunter.' Finding myself reluctant to impede the flow of the conversation I merely think, rather than say, 'But so are you', and anyway I know exactly why he says this, as he is a passionate observer and lover of birds of almost all kinds, with the exception of the corvine family (crows, rooks, jays, magpies and jackdaws – the relentless stealers of other birds' eggs and chicks). I have noticed on many occasions in my life before that men and women who are really keen hunters have a profound understanding and respect for wildlife. Richard's interests range across a wide spectrum of the natural world, and he is also commendably green. We both look down at the ground at Gilly, the black huntress-in-waiting, and I reckon that he is probably right – she could be a killer, but time will tell.

Karen, Lesley and Alex come up to look at the new addition to the household when they are passing on one of their walks, and I explain to Alex that I am hoping that Gilly will be able to go back to the breeders to one of their studs to have kittens when she comes into heat, or maybe the heat after that. Alex asks me nervously how long this might all take and I rather helplessly shrug my shoulders. I try to get Alex to nurse Gilly, but she yowks her disapproval at being picked up and cuddled, although, as ever, she purrs while she is complaining.

I email pictures of our new handful to Sue and get this response from her by return:

From: Sue
To: Marilyn
Sent: Wednesday, February 16, 6:54 pm
Subject: Re: !!!

Marilyn
Isn't she gorgeous!! I long to hear how you are getting on and if she's as bumptious as you say, then she will have the others under her thumb in very short order. At least now you will know what it's like living with a kitten hell-bent on LIVING LIFE to the full. Everyone thinks I exaggerate Georgie's exploits, but now you will know . . . The kittens will be very tempting I can see. As to my lot they all seem fine, perhaps a closer group now, it's difficult to know if I am making up their emotions or they are genuine, hard to say. Max and Johnnie seem to spend a lot more time together and Johnnie seems quite oblivious to the fact her sister has gone. Perhaps if Chatto hadn't been so old and always the loner it would have been different. And as I look round the room, pictures hanging askew, bits of paper everywhere, cushion in the middle of the floor and my recycled paper bin

turned upside down, then no change in Georgie either . . .

Sue

Back at the Coach House all is not completely well with the other three cats, but Michael and I are reasonably sanguine about this, as it is very early days, and Gilly is stronger meat than they have yet had to contemplate, so she is bound to take some getting used to. The bed-time ritual has become one of the tensest moments of the day, as pre-Gilly the three cats would all sit on the bed until we put the lights out and then one by one go back downstairs, although sometimes Titus would stay either on the bed or in the neighbouring bathroom on a cushion on the floor. The situation now is that Fannie and Gilly are at such daggers drawn that Gilly wins out and Fannie is beginning not even to come into the room for that last precious cuddle. Pushkin and Titus come into the room but are somewhat uneasy in Gilly's presence. Gilly sleeps on our bed all night every night and that is that.

Early one evening, just as I am starting to prepare supper, the phone goes and it is Jeff on the other end. He tells me Lesley has brought her kitten Joey back from Manchester. She and her boyfriend had been having problems with him in their tiny flat and they just felt they couldn't give him enough exercise so Lesley has, with some regret, decided that he will have a much better life having his freedom to run and play in Hutton Roof and she will at least see him at weekends. This means that they won't now be able to take a kitten from me.

'Jeff, it is great for Joey and of course I understand and Joey is a lucky boy. I imagine that Alex is thrilled, isn't she?'

'Yes, she is very happy to have him home, and it's better for him, without a doubt.'

'Well, anyway we are a long way off getting young Gilly pregnant, so it's fine with us.'

In fact, since the introduction of the little black bundle to the inner sanctum of the Coach House, a bundle who perpetually triggers the question 'Where the devil is she now?' or sometimes by Michael, who is deeply infatuated by the little madam, 'Where's Black Magic, it's too quiet?' the now seemingly enormous, adult feline residents are variously put out. As ever, Titus, the most benign

and the most amiable of the three cats, is the least
disrupted and, also being the most selfish, has been
at some pains to maintain her sleep station in the
armchair in my study, which is the only room that's
guaranteed to be warm during the daytime. In spite
of all manner of trials to her composure put up by
the young scallywag she has resisted them all and
simply turns her back on whatever provocation she
is offered and continues to sleep in the armchair.
Occasionally, very occasionally, she will hiss at
Gilly, or clock her one with her front leg, but
mainly she just keeps her head down, literally and
metaphorically.

Pushkin, on the other hand, is more seriously
alarmed by the black kitten and regularly growls at
her as much as she growls at him. He mainly avoids
her, but at certain times during the day
he will be involved in a hectic game
of chase in which she,
always, chases
him, violently
and frantic-
ally, all over
the house,

up and down
both flights
of stairs until he
finally finds some high place
of retreat. However, there is an
early sign that this is about to
change. I noticed this morning that it
was Pushkin chasing Gilly and they
were both clearly enjoying it, so
perhaps a real friendship will develop here.

Fannie and Gilly together are more of a
worriment. Gilly has a way of staring at Fannie that
is quite unnerving, even to me, but the effect it has
on Fannie is explosive. When Gilly decides to 'do'
her stare she is usually crouching, or sitting. I have
never seen her 'look the look' standing up. It is a
steady unwavering look with barely a blink to be
seen and is directed at Fannie and only at Fannie.
When Fannie sees this she becomes visibly
agitated, and will unconsciously lick her nose. She
hunches down in a crouching position and to begin
with she growls. She follows her growl with hissing
which becomes increasingly intense and then she
makes her mistake. She runs. Gilly chases. Fannie

panics. If she cannot get away she will crouch low down on the floor with her head close to the ground and her ears fully back against her head, in a combination of full submission and complete aggression, hissing as if her life depends upon it. As Gilly closes in on her she will jump up and leap over Gilly and run. Often in this part of the chase Gilly will get very close to Fannie and the combined noise from both of them is terrible to hear. We keep finding lumps of Fannie's fur at the top of the stairs where Gilly has managed to catch up with her just to give her a nip out of the back of her thigh. She hasn't yet drawn blood but I live in fear of this.

Within three weeks of Gilly joining us we meet and start a friendship with a young couple called Mark and France. France is a French Canadian schoolteacher who teaches French at a school in Bristol and who, as a hobby, undertakes feline portraits as commissions. She is a very talented draughtswoman, as I am to discover. They arrive with us around lunchtime one day near the end of February and are both bemused by Gilly's antics, although France expresses some concern about the reaction of Fannie to Gilly's 'bullying'. We talk of many things and I discover that she and Mark have no children but share their lives very happily with four cats, called Apollo, Spooky, Grippette and Uni, all of whom I hope to meet in the future.

In the course of our talk France admits to me that she is hoping yet again that Spooky, who remains her only entire cat, will have a litter of kittens later in the year. She never stops her or encourages her, but leaves her to find her stud as she will and when she will. I also speak of my hopes for Gilly and her kittens.

'You could have your hands full with that one,' France laughs as we watch Gilly chasing Fannie upstairs yet again.

CHAPTER 9

I have dwelt with some enthusiasm on the subject of our new scamp, Gilly, and her relationship with the resident adult felines, but still hanging over us is the spectre that the almost-realised dream of living up here may be shattered and we shall have to return South, complete with cats, to a housebound life again. Already the cold wind of financial ruin is blowing around our ankles as eleven months on we are still paying out on two mortgages. Michael is continuing to have problems with the renter and a possible sale of Moon Cottage seems to be as elusive as ever. The property market in the South remains as static as it was at the end of last year. Following a viewing in early January, some serious interest in the cottage was expressed by a couple to our neighbour Shirley, who showed them round. They remained very keen until on their next viewing they brought their very tall teenaged son from their house in Central London. As he entered the cottage, Michael who had decided he better go down for this himself afterwards told me, he ducked and visibly hated it. The beamed ceilings downstairs are very low, it must be admitted, but I also suspect that the lad may well have not wanted to leave the bright lights and the stimulation of his metropolitan friends.

As well as complaining about everything under the sun, the woman who is renting the place, having initially agreed to allow one viewing a week by any potential purchaser, starts to be difficult about that too and as a result we fail to show the cottage to a couple from Shepherd's Bush who had sounded very interested. There have been one or two other desultory viewings too, but they have come to nothing. Michael and I hardly dare to speak to each other on the subject of the cottage – it is becoming a forbidden topic laced with mutual recrimination. One night, however, I am profoundly disturbed by the sound of Michael sobbing heavily. As I turn towards him I find that he is crying in his sleep, but when I do wake him from what I hope is just a bad dream, for dreaming he was, I discover that in waking too he is torn apart by the fear that all our savings are evaporating and without jobs and incomes we have a bleak outlook in store. I try to reassure him all will be well, but I know my reassurance has a hollow ring.

The most healing thing I know is having a cuddle with the cats, and I long for Michael to find peace in that way. He does interact with them, a great deal, but it is more through conversations than touch, although Titus sits on him often. For me it is Fannie who has that magic touch. I can feel stress leaving me with every breath when she is in my arms. I had a powerful email on just this subject from Shirani. Her mother died from a tumour and she was utterly stricken by her death. At this terrible time, although she received love and help from her husband and family, it was the silent help of the cats that seemed to be most healing:

From: Shirani Fernando-Bradford
To: Marilyn Edwards

What amazed me was the compassion that Lucky and Barnaby, my two cats, showed to me . . . If I cried, Lucky would come and sit next to me and put her tiny paw on my hand to comfort me. Barnaby would be near me but there was very little physical contact.

Until one night I had a terrible nightmare about Mum, I awoke so suddenly and I know I didn't make a sound. I didn't even sit up. Barnaby was sleeping at the bottom of the bed. Suddenly, I felt him walk the entire length of my body, and he lay on my chest . . . He put his head on my left shoulder and cuddled me purring gently till I went back to sleep. I find cats every bit as compassionate as people, and sometimes more so because of their sensitivity to emotional changes.

🐾 🐾 🐾

This coming Thursday Fannie is booked in for her hysterectomy. She has been intermittently on heat again since the abrupt end of her phantom pregnancy and she is becoming increasingly loud when she is calling, so we are both really glad that the date has arrived at last.

Yet again we have to go through the nil-by-mouth business with all four cats even though only Fannie is to be subjected to the horrors of surgery, and a restless and complaining sort of night is had by all. In the morning, with dark rings under my eyes, I scoop Fannie up to put her in the cat cage. Just before I do, Michael reaches across and, gently fondling her ear, says with real sadness in his voice:

'Fannie, Fannie, Fannie – I can't bear that you aren't going to have any kittens. You would have made such beautiful kittens and you would have

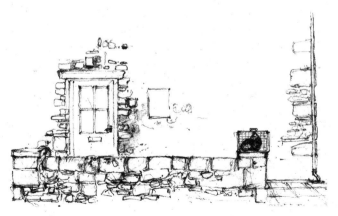

been such a good mother.' He's right, dammit.

I drive off to the vet's with a heavy heart. It goes without saying that I am, as ever, terrified of the actual procedure. Gerard, always understanding, takes receipt of her and assures me that there is nothing to worry about. I don't help matters by introducing the thought that as she is a tortoiseshell and therefore more highly strung than her sister, Titus, she is more likely to panic in recovery. He smiles his beatific smile and says:

'Marilyn, just phone me around midday, and I will be able to tell you then she has had the operation and I'll be able to give you a time to collect her.' I throw back a wobbly smile at him gratefully and potter off. I mess around all morning, unable to settle down to anything, but before it is time for me to phone him, the phone goes and it's Gerard's voice. He is so good, because before I can get into a further panic he just says very calmly and precisely:

'She's had her operation and she is just coming round nicely now. She needs another hour or two down here, but you can come down at about 2 p.m. and collect her then.' I issue a silent prayer of thanks and start my first proper work of the day. After I get Fannie back home I am delighted that the other cats do not hiss and spit at her in the way that she always hisses and spits at them post-operatively. Titus gives one token hiss but very quickly accepts her completely. Fannie's recovery is immediately faster than that of Titus, but Gerard did say that he had an almighty struggle removing Titus's uterus which was not the case with the much slimmer Fannie, and what happens on the operating table is directly connected to the manner of recovery.

It is thought by some veterinary surgeons that physiologically pain in humans and their companion animals is the same but that the intellectual knowledge that pain is about to be inflicted (in the case, say, of a woman voluntarily undergoing hysterectomy) can make the perception of pain much greater for the human. It appears that animal patients recover much faster than humans enduring the same procedure. Animals seem to be back to their pre-operative activity levels within days, sometimes hours, whereas it can take weeks for humans to recover to the same degree. On the other hand, it is also surprisingly difficult to read an animal's response to pain as in the wild an animal that manifests its pain will become vulnerable to its many potential predators, so it may well post-operatively sit quietly without any observable indication that it is experiencing pain. Sometimes veterinary care staff or clinicians may mistake this as 'resting comfortably'. Instead, this is more likely an instinctive response for survival. Gerard, however, is superb at detecting pain in animals and although I thought I knew Titus well, it was he who picked up her arthritic pain in her back legs and he knew that she was uncomfortable after his hysterectomy on her. Fannie is showing little sign of discomfort. On her return home she goes upstairs with a little difficulty, but she manages it and lies down on the chair in my study and sleeps, and the following day she appears to be back to normal although I am sure she must be feeling some pain. Outwardly the only visible sign of what she has undergone is a large neat scar on her flank surrounded by a large square of white shaven flesh, which she ignores for the main part. Gerard is a master at concealed internal stitching and none of my cats have needed to wear collars post-operatively.

For some time now there has been a cooling down of the strong bond that has existed since birth between Fannie and Titus. I'm not certain what has caused it, but from my diary entries I suspect it started around the time of Fannie's 'phantom' pregnancy and was then exacerbated by the spaying of Titus. I find I have not wanted to acknowledge this rift as their closeness was such a key part of their relationship with each other and possibly because I am fearful that this breakdown has been caused by my intervention. They still occasionally allogroom, but almost always now it ends in 'tears' with Titus getting quite cross with Fannie and biting her or putting her paws round her throat and then one or other of them flounces off. Fannie usually shuns Titus and whereas they had always previously shared the armchair in my study, only one of them now sleeps in it at any one time.

Pushkin maintains his distance from Fannie, although he gave her hindquarters a sound sniffing on her return from the vet's, but he still follows Titus around doggedly, when he is awake that is. He especially likes to follow her down to the feeding station (it is almost as if unwittingly she signals to him that that is where she is going) and probably rather irritatingly to her he will walk back and forth in front of whichever bowl she is aiming for. He watches Gilly with what seems to be increasingly keen attention, although that is hardly surprising as Gilly is, of course, a young pre-pubescent female and therefore definitely interesting to a male cat, even if neutered.

Gilly continues to chase all of them. Mainly she is trying to play, but some of it appears to be an assertion of dominance. Her stare is overpowering, even to me, and she does a lot of that. She also talks a great deal. I would even say shouts. She talks about going out. She talks about having bowel movements. She talks about her food; about having it and also about not having it. She talks about being picked up. She talks about not being picked up. She talks to closed windows and to closed doors a lot and I have had to beg Michael not to respond by opening them, as I learned a long time ago that cats will miaow remorselessly for things they want, and you will become their complete slave, once they learn that vocal demands are met. So far it has worked with Gilly too. If she sits silently by the door she gets let out, if she makes a racket she doesn't.

There are some early signs of our Northern Spring burgeoning forth, but March is a treacherous month and can change at any moment. February was very wet and mild, but recently we have had a cold spell and now, suddenly, there is warm sunshine and I have just seen an early bumblebee. A couple of nights ago I could hear frogs croaking fit to bust and I am sure it is the males beginning to come in to fertilise our females. The horse chestnut tree is in leaf and the blue tits have been nesting for some time now. The dawn chorus has been building up day by day and it is on close to full voltage now and, although I am not sure if there is a connection, the owls seem especially noisy at night too. There is a day of wonderful sunshine and Michael and I walk up the crags. Near the top we turn round and look back down and across to the two Yorkshire Peaks of Whernside and Ingleborough and the Barbon fells and then turn at an angle of 90° in a northerly direction to look across to the high hills of the Lake District. After a bit more walking and scrambling we reach the summit and look down in a south-westerly direction where we can glimpse the shimmer of water that is the distant Morecambe Bay. We have just looked over a part of the three counties of North Yorkshire, Cumbria and Lancashire – counties which Michael always refers to as 'God's own country'. Michael puts his arm round my shoulders and I squeeze his hand. We don't need to say anything, we know it is paradise. We sit down back to back for support and look out at the far horizons and we both, completely simultaneously, let out huge sad sighs, which acts of melodrama make us giggle helplessly.

CHAPTER 10

Meanwhile, life goes on at the Coach House. As spring surges forth in fits and starts both the birdlife and the vole, mouse and shrew life start to multiply too. The four cats, who through long dark wet February have been content to stay mainly indoors, are now trying to get out into the open air from early in the morning and stay out there. Fannie is the most virulent hunter and kills her prey very quickly. Since Gilly has joined the household Fannie has if anything increased her kill-rate. Small mammals, rather than birds, tend to be her chosen quarry. When they are outside Gilly watches Fannie with a controlled respect that is quite different from her behaviour with Fannie inside the house. She may be consciously learning. Her own mother would never have had the chance to teach her hunting skills in the open air with live prey as they were all contained within the house. Pushkin is probably the next most prolific hunter and, as with most cats, he has that tenacious and slightly terrifying ability to stare for many minutes at a time at some potential victim who in the end just has to move, being unable to sustain immobility any longer. Titus of the three is now the least active as a hunter, which may be because she is lazy or more likely because she finds fast movement difficult. She hunts and kills if something offers itself up to her, without her needing to move very much.

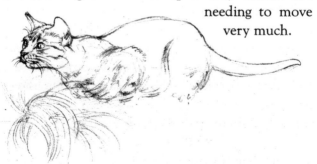

Today Fannie catches a wood mouse,[9] which she despatches quickly but, before I can stop her and to my immense surprise, she starts to eat it, very quickly and while I, and the three other cats I might say, look on with our mouths hanging open, the head and body are no more. All that remains are the feet and a tail. Fannie will barely eat wet cat food and certainly not any fresh food raw or cooked, so what stimulus suddenly caused this behaviour, natural in a predator but not anything I have known Fannie to do earlier, I cannot properly say. Titus, Pushkin and Gilly come forward to sniff the remains and then saunter off. Perhaps it was establishing some form of ownership or authority on Fannie's part.

When the cats are outside I am able to get the three adult ones in fairly easily, by shouting 'In! In!' loudly, or at worst by going out and catching them individually and carrying them back in my arms, but Gilly is completely impossible to corral and, at

---

[9] aka field mouse (Apodemus sylvaticus).

the slightest suggestion that the time has come, she will hide for long periods under the garden shed, where she is beyond reach until she and she alone chooses to return in. Gilly is, however, adorable, although she still hates to be picked up and one of the things she does if she is really trying to get away is to stretch herself out rigid in my arms, which is apparently a very 'Bengal' thing to do. When I nurse her on her back in my arms she makes a long low guttural complaining sort of moan, which she can keep up for a long time. It is very funny. She also emits wind when being picked up, but so pungently that you have to be strong to withstand

the smell. She loves to be stroked which makes her purr really loudly. As her fur is the softest in the world and she is shiny black, she gets stroked a lot and being purred at is very rewarding. She is a very person-oriented cat and follows either Michael or me around the house doggedly and likes to lie down near to wherever each of us is. Her breeders have put me in touch with Beth, a friend of theirs, who acquired a melanistic Bengal from them a year earlier, called Treacle. I talk to Beth and she reassures me on the wind and loose bowel movement front:

'Treacle did that too, but his tummy settled down once he was on grown-up food. He was a greedy pig and wouldn't eat his own food, thinking Teddy's[10] grown-up food was quite delicious. Thankfully, it suited him down to the ground and the farting pretty much ceased. It was disconcerting to be nasally assaulted every time that we picked him up. Enjoy your Gilly.'

---

[10] As well as Treacle, Beth and Steve share their lives with Teddy, another Bengal and Lulu a half-cross Bengal together with two dogs, Suzie, a Border Collie cross, and Griff, a mongrel collie.

Shortly after this, however, Treacle has to have an operation for the vet to try to find an undescended testicle,[11] which is causing problems and Beth writes of her fears on that day with an exquisite eloquence:

> We had an early start to our day today. Treacle has gone to Thornhill, to the vet's. I feel very wobbly and it will be a long day.
>
> I don't know how well I would take it, should Treacle be one of those cats that doesn't come out from the anaesthetic.
>
> Treacle is anachronistic – the ever-present shadow that brings light into our lives. He is always there. Just 'there'. Just 'present'. He's not fussy; he will lap-sit sometimes, but generally just sits about six inches away on the desk (right of keyboard) – with that amazingly long and prehensile tail elegantly swathed about his front paws. Just . . . Sitting . . . and Being Black, with amber eyes watching our activities with a deep and abiding interest. There is a hole in my life

---

[11] unilateral cryptorchidism.

today. A piece of me is missing. I can't even begin to think about it becoming a permanent one. We had a Siamese once, who Didn't Make It. So I wobble. Until 4 p.m.

He did make it, thank goodness, but he was a sore boy, who removed most of his stitches and ended up with a collar. And then Beth tells me:

Poor Treacle – I promised him his collar was coming off today – and now because it isn't healing properly they need to investigate and he will have more stitches! He clawed the final three stitches out, by the way. He's a bad, bad cat! Treacle has discovered why he keeps Human slaves. He's constantly pushing his face up for scratching and saying, 'It's your fault, you do it!' He bites our finger ends if he doesn't get his own way. It's really charming, this collared but determined face looking up and demanding a scratch.

Beth's eloquent utterance, 'There is a hole in my life today. A piece of me is missing', is hauntingly witnessed in the grief felt by Dedde for his companion Duff as expressed here by Anette Nyberg[12]

— — —

From: Anette Nyberg
To: Marilyn Edwards
Sent: 21 March 17:01
Subject: Re: The Cats of Moon Cottage

Dear Marilyn,
Strange you should say you think that Otto's death triggered Septi's cancer. My first cat Duff (a beautiful black girl with the loveliest personality you can imagine) grew up with Dedde (a tabby boy who was 'all purrs'). They were as close as two cats can be that aren't brother and sister. When Duff got ill and I had to take her to the vet one final time Dedde was heart-broken . . . didn't want to eat much (he loved food before) and nearly didn't purr . . .

---

[12] who lives in a deeply remote part of Sweden with her two current feline companions, Lisa and Maja.

For Dedde it seemed that once his companion in life, the one he 'loved', was no longer there to share his life, it was as if he didn't want to live any more . . . Before this he was fine, playing and purring as always, but that changed when Duff died. I sometimes could see the pain in his eyes and also that 'the spark' if you like was fading away . . . and indeed so was he.

I talked to the vet about it and he said he was sure that animals can grieve in just the same way that humans can. Dedde didn't have anything seriously wrong with him that a diet couldn't sort out, but when he was left alone he deteriorated fast . . . I'm sure he wanted to die, the sad thing was having to watch this lovely cat just let go of his will to live . . .

One day I found him in the kitchen by the fridge door, and there are no words to describe the look on his beautiful face as I realised that he had "wet" himself, the poor little cat. I then realised that I could no longer postpone that trip to the vet. There was no reason to make him suffer any longer, and I called the vet and a close friend who offered to go with us. It is quite a long drive to where the vet is, 90 kilometres to be precise, but this day it went so fast . . . and all the time as I drove there I was thinking that soon he will no longer be with

111

us, but with his much-loved Duff instead.

It was such a sad goodbye, but I was sure as I held him in my arms that he was much better off without the humiliation and constant grief. There and then ended the life of a wonderful cat and I'm quite sure that a part of me died there too.

I felt as if I didn't want to go on without my 2 dearest friends for 14 years, and as soon as anyone tried to mention that perhaps a kitten would make me smile again I remembered thinking: I don't think I'll ever smile again and that I just didn't want to replace them, ever . . . But as you know yourself things can change, the pain and loss is not as bad anymore, but these two are always in my heart because they gave me so much.

I believe that much-loved cats leave an essence or impression behind them that might have to do with all the strong feelings and love, after all, is energy, isn't it?

Yours,

Anette, Lisa and Maja

🐈 🐈 🐈

After a long silence, on 7 March we receive the following announcement from the internet agency which is selling Moon Cottage.

From: info@halfapercent.com
To: Marilyn Edwards
Sent: Monday, March 07, 3:51 PM
Subject: Viewing Request

Dear Marilyn
I have two applicants interested in viewing your property, see below.

Appointments
Saturday 12 March 12:30
Saturday 12 March 13:30

Please let me know what days and times that you can do, if you are unable to do the above days and times.
  Regards,
  Viewings Department
  1/2% – Halfapercent.com

We scurry around to make arrangements for the two viewings. One is to be done by a local agent and the other by our saintly neighbour, Shirley.

Our renter on this occasion accommodates us by allowing these appointments. Michael and I are wary of getting too excited, we have been here so many times before, but all the same our hearts are beating faster and we spend the next few days doing some distracted nail biting. I manage to have a phone conversation with Caroline, one half of the couple wanting the second appointment who, like her partner Nathan, is a medical research scientist working in Central London and who both, it transpires, now want to live further out. I explain to her that there is a 360 degrees virtual tour of the cottage which, if she has the patience to let it download, she can view online on the Halfapercent website and she says she will try to get into it. She has already been on the website for some time studying the stills.

Saturday 12 March comes at last. The first couple are again worried by the low ceilings and decide that it is not for them, but Shirley phones us to tell us that Caroline and Nathan, the second appointment, like the cottage very much indeed. Later that weekend Nathan and Caroline phone us and tell us themselves how much they love it and then, heart-stoppingly, they make an offer. It is inevitably below our asking price and with some trepidation we negotiate a compromise and suddenly Michael and I, to our tearful near-disbelief, find we have agreed a sale.

On Monday morning I receive this email from Caroline:

– – –

From: Caroline Wallace
To: Marilyn Edwards
Sent: Monday, March 14, 10:07 AM
Subject: RE: Moon cottage

Dear Marilyn,

I haven't been able to sleep since Saturday. I just keep thinking about the cottage and how wonderful it is! I completely understand that it must have been a real wrench for you to leave such a beautiful place. If the cottage picks its owners, then it certainly worked its charms on my husband. I already knew that I would love it but Nathan had some concerns about the busy road and the lack of off-street parking. However, after about

2 minutes in the cottage he was more excited than I have ever seen him.

I have been in touch with Halfapercent . . . and they will contact you today . . . The couple who came to see our flat on Saturday seemed very keen. I will keep you fully informed of our progress with the sale of our own flat.

Thank you very much for your kindness.

I'll be in touch soon.

Best wishes,

Caroline

Dr Caroline Wallace

CHAPTER 11

In the middle of all the wonderful things that are happening around Moon Cottage, I receive this note. Letters from other cat lovers frequently bear tidings of joy or heartache, and sometimes both, but on a few occasions they just stop you in your tracks completely:

— — —

From: Emma
To: Marilyn Edwards
Sent: Thursday, March 31, 10:09 AM

My cat died four years ago and I don't think I'll ever 'get over it' properly and I can't face having another cat. She died in her sleep, on my bed – something awoke me early in the morning and I looked at her curled up by my feet. She was twitching slightly, so I stroked her, thinking she was having a nightmare. But she never woke up and I was, and remain, heart-broken.

However, I just thought I'd pass this story on to you, which I heard from an RSPCA worker called Diana Lewis who works (or used to) for the North Devon Branch. She was called to a house to look after a cat whose owner had died. The owner was an old man and he had collapsed on the floor. When the ambulance arrived they found his face was sopping wet and the cat was on top of him, frantically licking his face, trying to revive him.

As the cat was also old, the RSPCA lady took the cat home with her to look after him, as she thought it would be kinder. He was very subdued and curled up into a ball, and wouldn't respond to any attention. The RSPCA lady left him alone and the next day went to stroke him; except he had died in the night.

Isn't that sad? A cat who died of a broken heart.

Emma

* * *

Following the news from Caroline and Nathan that they really do want to buy Moon Cottage, Michael and I hardly know ourselves. To feel the tension lifting off us is like the best holiday in the world. We know we mustn't relax completely, as they will, of course, have to have a full survey done on it and it is a very old building so that could throw up any number of problems. It is so lovely, though, to know that they feel the same way about Moon Cottage as we did and do, and, before us, Janet and any number of other people to whom Moon Cottage has opened herself up. Moon Cottage chooses who lives within her walls and it never happens until she is ready. We make a date to go down and meet Caroline and Nathan in April.

I hear Michael addressing the cats as he lets them out into the sharp spring air for their first early morning romp of the day:

'There you go, you lucky lot, you don't have to be confined within the walls of Moon Cottage after all. Enjoy your paradise here, go on, run, run! And mind that traffic!'

'Oh, don't even joke on that subject!' I urge him, as I give him a hug. We both walk out into the garden. The hills are white with snow. Our end of the village is up on a hill but we are surrounded by even higher hills to the West, the North and the East and these have been covered with snow for some days now. Each time that the great Ingleborough looks as if its snowy cape is getting a bit threadbare and the dark stone starts showing through, there is another snowfall and yet again she is cloaked in immaculate white. I shiver as I look out at our splendid vista.

'Soon the lambs are going to be born and it is so hard when it's like this for them.'

'But Mo, tomorrow it could just as easily be sunny again, with a big thaw and you said yourself a few days ago that spring is well under way.' And sure enough that is exactly what happens. There is a switch in temperature, a thaw sets in, and lambs start popping out from everywhere. Five days later, as we look out over our gate into the field behind our little paddock across the road, we can see the newly born lambs wiggling their tails in that wonderful lambkin way as they head-butt their long-suffering mothers in search of milk. I had asked Richard Prickett, whose lambs they are, what breed they were and he replied mainly Texels but with a few Texel/Cheviot crosses and I think he also said Lleyns. I love lambing time; it is my most favourite time of year in the farming calendar, although in the old days hay time came a close second. The only trouble is that in the North there is almost always what they call 'lamb snow', which is the inevitable late winter snowfall that comes during lambing or immediately after they are born, and it is a terrible strain on the endurance of both the tiny lambs and their mothers, not to mention the harassed shepherds in whose care they are.

Today a group of 'pilgrims' turn up next door, at the Old Vicarage, to call on Annabel and Richard to borrow the key to the church, so that they may go and visit the place where the Reverend Theodore Bayley Hardy V.C., D.S.O., M.C.[13] was the incumbent until 1918, when he was wounded on the Somme and died of his wounds in a military

---

[13] For more info there is a very good biography called *It's Only Me*, A life of The Reverend Theodore Bayley Hardy, V.C., D.S.O., M.C. Vicar of Hutton Roof, Westmorland by David Raw (Frank Peter's Publishing, 1988) ISBN 0948511451.

hospital in Rouen three weeks before the Armistice. The Reverend Hardy, with the beautiful face of a poet, was the most decorated non-combatant of the First World War. This man was very brave and very good, and it makes me ache to think that we live in the house which was his coach house, although his favourite mode of transport was his bicycle, which in itself says much about the man. Michael and I have cycled round here only once and it almost killed us! It is excellent that people do come to seek him and his living out, but I wish more people knew about him, he was a remarkable man.

Spring is now seriously under way. The dawn chorus which I had thought was at its most incandescent two weeks ago is now utterly overwhelming and I am awestruck at the performance that our feathered choir lays on in its collective passion for love and life. It starts before sunrise at around 5.30 a.m. and builds until it is near impossible for anyone to sleep on through it and, however cold the weather, or fierce the winds, the birds are in no way discouraged, but riotously follow their instinct to acquire and protect their territory and attract and keep their mate. I cannot remember a better one. On top of this there are the frogs. Well, more precisely it is the frogs who are on top of the frogs. For the last two days I have seen two pairs of frogs firmly attached to each other and letting go for nothing and no one. The last twenty-four hours have been very windy and wet and mild, which is a total change from the weather hitherto. Michael comes bouncing into the bathroom with a pair of field glasses, gurgling, because today there are no fewer than ten frogs in the pond. This is slightly mad as the pond is nothing like large enough to cope with ten frogs. By lunchtime there are three enormous clumps of frogspawn, almost covering the entire surface of the pond. It really is so much that I wonder if I should not take some out, but on investigation I discover that, however much is laid, such a tiny fraction of it will develop into adult frogs that statistically speaking I should leave the whole lot, so I do. Unlike last summer when the frogs in our pond would let us bend down and stroke them (for fun I did try, just once, to kiss one of them but he wouldn't let me), these frogs submerge the second we open the door, so I am sure that means they have migrated some distance for the spawning and don't know us. The volume and constancy of their croaking seem almost exotic. Further proof, should proof be needed, of spring's arrival is provided by no fewer than three bumblebees flying slowly around the garden, low down to the ground, looking for nest sites I imagine.

We are keeping the cats in because someone told me that Bengals are particularly keen on frogs, but I suspect Bengals are keen on anything and everything. With great difficulty Michael and I have clipped Gilly's claws; they were lethal and so long they were beginning to grow inwards.

Fannie has started to sleep up on top of the

bookcase which is the first time since we have been at the Coach House, but it is awkward for her to get up to it. She always slept on top of the high bookcases at Moon Cottage. Today, however, Gilly came into the room, saw where Fannie was and, although much clumsier than Fannie (her sense of balance is still not as good as that of the other cats), she managed to climb up and challenge Fannie. Fannie was distraught and although she hissed and spat, she finally capitulated and half jumped, half fell down. So far there is no indication at all that the hormonal change since her hysterectomy has made her any more relaxed. She seems to be progressively more nervous and withdrawn. Since this episode Fannie has discovered an old leather-covered laundry box that I use for filing things, which is sitting on top of my filing cabinet. She can get into it by leaping off the top of the library steps, as long as I remember to leave them in front of the filing cabinet – not very convenient – but I desperately need her to find somewhere she can feel safe and high. I have put her favourite blanket in it and that is where she has been sleeping ever since.

Gilly and Pushkin continue to play together

quite a bit. Sometimes he runs away because they are playing chase, but comes back for more, but sometimes he runs away and hides. Often though I spot him just sitting very still, watching her, almost obsessively. She appears not to notice that he is doing this, but as she is both female and a signed-up member of the genus Felis Catus she is almost certainly aware of him. Michael shocked me the other day as he was watching her cross the garden towards the gate:

'Gilly is such a girl somehow – look at her!'

'What on earth do you mean?'

'She is just so feminine. She sort of wiggles knowingly as she struts out – look see she is doing it now!'

'Michael, for goodness sake, she's a blimming cat.' He laughed. All the same I do sort of see what he means. Pushkin now sleeps on top of the bathroom cupboard if Fannie and Titus aren't there – otherwise on the blue blanket inside the wardrobe in the guest bedroom and only when he is really cold on the vet blanket on the cushions on the floor in my study. Titus spends her time alternating between the top of the same bathroom cupboard, but not if Pushkin is there, and the armchair in my study. Gilly has now taken over Pushkin's old bed on top of the box on the floor in my study. Her baby igloo is in the box, but for the moment she is shunning that during the daytime, although I think she sleeps on it at night.

Of the four cats, I would say that Fannie and Pushkin seem to be the most unsettled. Gilly and Titus both appear to have pretty much the same agenda, which is to do it their way, where and when they want to and ideally in the warmest spot.

CHAPTER 12

April blows in cold and fierce and, true to form, we watch a few large flakes of snow come floating down, although not enough to merit the title 'lamb snow'. As I peer down into our pond I see the tiniest wiggling of the tadpoles flexing their tails still suspended in their jelly and some way off free swimming.

Anne, our sub-postmistress, has resurrected her scarecrow down in her field with her hens, her duck and her goat, and a very striking scarecrow she is. I am curious, though, to know why this elegant, dark-haired, slim but curvaceous 'lovely' with black hair and one eye open and one eye closed, hugely lashed, wearing a tight-fitting red polo-necked jumper atop a smart black and white checked skirt complete with black tights, has suddenly been put on duty in her field, so the next time I remember I ask her about the young wench in her scarlet top.

'Ah ha! Well, she's there because of those damned buzzards. I have some newly hatched chicks and those hawks are the very devil for going after them . . . and the kestrels are nearly as bad and it helps to keep them off the hen food anyway.' I also discover that one day shortly after Ms S. Crow took up her station in the field the venerable Jimmy, a veteran Hutton Roofer, passing by on his mobility scooter to start the long climb up the hill for his daily chat to his much-loved wife at her grave in the churchyard, stopped his vehicle at Anne's wall and with some concern in his voice called out across the field towards the scarecrow, which, was at this point standing, or rather sloping, at a bit of a drunken lean:

'Anne, Anne, are you alright? Anne, answer me, why are you leaning like that?' and the real Anne, hearing him calling, had to go out and reassure him she was fit and well, but she was delighted to see that her doppelganger had done her job so well.

'Mind you,' Anne grins wickedly, 'the scarecrow I had some years back was her, but in a somewhat different rig-out. Before she had more what I call the look of Dolly Parton about her and a bigger bust. She was blonde in those days. It was to scare off the foxes. This time round I dyed her hair black and made her slimmer.' I laugh but when I go back and really study the mouth and the eyes I realise that she bears more than a passing resemblance to Dolly Parton, she's the spitting image.

'So it's a busty blonde to scare off Mr Fox and a slim brunette for the mighty buzzard, is it?' Anne makes no reply, she just smiles enigmatically. Then she adds:

'Talking of that other scarecrow, did you hear about the foxes and what happened?'

'No, tell, tell.'

'It was awful – it was the middle of winter and very cold, and being out late I hadn't got back to shut the hens in and those foxes, they came and cleared off with all the fat ones, the ones that were laying. They left just six of the scrawniest behind.

The remains of dead chickens and ducks were spread all round the village. You know, those released urban foxes are the bad ones: they come when it is only just dusk; the rural ones are much more timid and would wait until the middle of the night. That's why I made the scarecrow. I wrote a poem about it.' This is an extract:

Tales of a Postmistress

. . .

Oh! How did she remember,
One frosty night last December.
Her hens and ducks that fox did find.
How he and his pals had dined!

Headless bodies scattered throughout the village,
What a senseless, wasteful pillage.
. . .
Meanwhile the postmistress sits and thinks:
'That fox I must hoodwink,
Before its teeth in my remaining hens it sinks.'
Suddenly up she jumps and says, 'Ah! Yes I know.'
Off up to her husband's shed she did go
Busy with wood, hammer, nail and hay
Until the end of the long day.
A lady scarecrow was in progress
With blonde hair, black stockings and red dress.
Out of this shed the lady came.
With her winking eyes, she looked game.
In the postmistress's paddock she stood
Amongst all those hens, ducks and mud.
Now one day when the postmistress was away
A little game village folks thought they would play.
Returned she did when it was night,
To find the scarecrow's bloomers had changed
from blue to white!
Her black stockings she was flashing.
Her position was one of inviting passion!
In her belt was tucked her dress.

Oh! She did look a mess.
Every day her positions changed
Till the postmistress nearly went deranged.

Meanwhile in the P.O. the village joker came to say:
'Now you will have Family Allowance to pay. . .
Your scarecrow is in the family way!'

© Anne Huntington, December 1995

🐧 🐧 🐧

Michael and I go down to Moon Cottage to meet Caroline and Nathan and to show them all the little things in the cottage that they need to know about. They are a charming couple and I know they are right for this special place. It is always horrible at this stage of selling a house, because you never know if it is going to be all right or if something terrible will still go wrong, but it feels so good being in the cottage with them. Wonderfully, too, Shirley has really warmed to them and they like Shirley, which helps no end. We owe Shirley so much for all that she has done and it would be so good if this couple turn out to be her new neighbours.

We return back North with our spirits high, but we discover that things are no better between the cats than they were when we left. Watching them closely suggests to me that the power is constantly shifting and they are all wary, I suspect mainly inspired by Gilly's explosive unpredictability. Pushkin seems to be losing a bit of weight and his fur has gone dull. He is such a timid cat that this could be a reaction to Gilly, or is he ailing? Unlike Fannie since her hysterectomy, he, since his castration, has become friendlier and much more touchy-feely with Michael, as well as me. I study him attentively. His eyes are bright and his nose is coldish. He seems alert enough, but this is by his standards of course – he still sleeps for four-fifths of every day. He has begun to chase Gilly more now. Usually he chases her after she chases him, but previously where he was inclined to run away and hide, now he simply turns around and gives back to her what she is dishing out. She seems to like it. I am sure that what is mostly motivating Gilly is a strong desire to play, but it seems not to be perceived in this way by the others. Pushkin still adores Titus but Titus, who is now gaining shocking amounts of weight since her spaying, seems to be on a short fuse with him and is quick to show her irritation. Titus will touch noses with Gilly but they never lie together as such. They will lie, by default, on the same large bed but not companionably. Pushkin and Gilly touch noses a little but Pushkin tends to be a bit jumpy which makes Gilly chase him and so he runs, although now he will chase her back again. Although I cannot say that it appears any better between Fannie and Gilly, Fannie does seem to be more relaxed with us.

Gilly really is one feisty cat. It would be anthropomorphic to suggest that she is deceitful when I don't know what it is that motivates her, but she appears to consciously lull the other cats into believing that she is in passive mode and is either paying them no attention at all, or certainly means no harm to them, but when they are totally relaxed she just goes for it. She will wait round the side of the sofa and then, when the others are displaying their wariness, she will look away, for really long periods. They will, eventually, visibly relax, at which point she swings round and attacks them.

Today she alarms me by jumping down the back of a large chest of drawers slotted into an alcove which is only 3¼ inches wider than the chest. The drawers are full and it is heavy and I simply can't move it. She gets stuck in the gap at the back and starts to panic and make a terrible fuss, but do what I may I'm unable to reach her. I try stuffing pillows down the back to try to get her to climb on to them and up that way, to no avail. I can hear her claws desperately scrabbling at the back of the slippery chest of drawers and eventually, in an almost morphing manner, she pulls herself in thin enough to squeeze through the crack at the side. I have no idea how she managed it and how her ribs survived it, but I am just praying that she will now leave it alone as a 'dangerous place'.

🐾 🐾 🐾

Caroline and Nathan contact us having had the results of their survey on Moon Cottage and, as expected, there is a long list of things that need attending to. The worst problem is damp which is inevitable in an old building, so we offer a contribution towards the cost of getting it fixed and agree a date for exchange and completion. We now feel able to take a longed-for holiday in France, but as usual I feel remorse and not a little apprehension about leaving the cats behind, especially not being certain of how Gilly is likely to react with the others over a fortnight. On the day we are to leave I bring out the hanging clothes holder as well as the big suitcase, as we are driving down to the south of France in our own car, and Titus, to my horror, takes one look at it and goes into a terrible hunched position of grief. She plonks her fat little self down on the still empty hanging clothes holder and just stays there. She refuses to move and, even when she hears the outside door open, she still stays there and will not go outside or anything. I try to comfort her but she is inconsolable. Fannie retires to my study and climbs up into her box which seems to be the only place in the whole house now where she feels really safe, as Gilly has usurped both the top of the cupboard in our bathroom and also the top of the bookshelves in my study but at the moment cannot get into the box on top of the filing cabinet. She keeps trying though, so it will only be a matter of time. Pushkin stays asleep in the spare bedroom and his body language remains inscrutable, so I have no idea if he feels any concern or not at our impending departure.

Kalyacitta, my stepdaughter, has very kindly agreed to cat-sit the house while we are away and some of the time she will have a girlfriend and also her partner, Vajragupta, to stay with her too.

We start our holiday in France happily enough, but after seven days away I am so nerve-wracked and anxious for news of the cats that finally I succumb and, just before we all retire to bed, I reckon it might be OK to phone KC and speak, so with a deep breath I dial our number back in Cumbria. She answers the phone almost immediately and seems content enough in herself, which is hugely reassuring, and I am much relieved. Eventually I feel able to broach the subject of the cats and Kalyacitta indicates that there is ongoing friction between Fannie and Gilly, although I could have expected nothing less.

'You never told me about Gilly's obsession with water, did you?' Kalyacitta laughingly chides me. 'I couldn't understand why near their water bowl in the conservatory I would mop up the puddle and then half an hour later it was as if the bowl was leaking, until I saw her paddling away in it, and today she went up to the pond and spent all her time in the corner by the rocks, and in the end she was standing in it.' It is so good to hear these small stories and after more in this vein I retire to bed comforted by the knowledge that they are in the safest hands it is possible to be.

While we are in France things suddenly start going wrong on the final stages of the sale of Moon Cottage, this time because the purchaser of Caroline and Nathan's flat is not prepared to exchange on the agreed date, and every other day we have fraught conversations with either Nathan and/or Caroline or our estate agent and the date is postponed yet again.

Under this cloud we make the long drive back home and finally we arrive back in Cumbria. Kalyacitta and Vajragupta say their farewells to us and KC assures us that she has loved being at the Coach House and tells us the cats are fine, which they self-evidently are. She tells me that Fannie killed a mouse, but that before she could clear it up it received a sky burial.[14] I laugh and hug myself with pleasure. She and VJ are both ordained Buddhists and so it is appropriate that a sky burial should happen for a mouse while they are both here.

Immediately we get back from holiday I receive an email from one of the youngest readers who has yet written to me. She deliciously signs herself 'From your biggest fans Kirsty and Merlin XXXXXXXXXXXXXXX'. Harriet aka Kirsty has a cat called Merlin and she gives me regular updates on his doings which are various and often very naughty. She has won a competition at school for a brilliant poem she wrote when she was eleven, which has now been published in a book she tells me. She is now twelve. I reproduce her winning

---

[14] sky burial is a ritual practice common in Tibet that involves placing the body of the deceased on high ground in a special place so that birds of prey will dispose of it, as many Tibetans believe that birds of prey are the carriers of souls to heaven.

poem 'A Wild Hack' and oh how I felt like that
when I was eleven too and utterly horse-mad:

A Wild Hack

Cantering, galloping, racing, trotting,
Over fields and through woods,
Flowing mane, flapping nostrils,
Through a puddle,
Over a log,

Stop for a picnic,
Run around, pick some flowers,
Calm down,
Lay on your back, stare at the clouds,
Wonder why??

Back to the stables,
Time to muck out,
Wished you were still out and about,
Got to go,
Back to the city,
Hoped it wasn't true!

© Harriet Garside

On 31 May we exchange contracts and on 9 June we complete the contract for the sale of Moon Cottage to Caroline and Nathan. We are weak with relief. We can hardly believe it has finally happened. Caroline and Nathan have two rabbits, one a female English Lop rabbit with those enormous ears, called Rosie, and the other, remarkably, a white Lionhead rabbit, called Scooter. I say 'remarkably', because Shirley also has a Lionhead rabbit called Buffy and saw this as a special sign that it was meant to be when Caroline and Nathan first saw the cottage. When we met Caroline and Nathan in Moon Cottage in April, Caroline had said:

'Let's raise a glass to Moon Cottage and also let's toast the Rabbits of Moon Cottage.' I long for Caroline to write *that* book. She writes me the following email in reply to my questions, and I am so glad I never knew about the Pinner property until now – phew!

From: Caroline Wallace
To: Marilyn Edwards
Cc: Nathan Richardson
Sent: Wednesday, June 22, 11:25 AM
Subject: RE: Moon Cottage

Dear Marilyn,

You asked about the cottage and the internet. I saw the cottage on the internet on 8 March and as you know we viewed it on 12 March. I had taken the 360 degree tour online but Nathan hadn't (he was really busy at work and tends not to get as obsessed as I do). I just knew I was going to love it. We arranged to see a 3 bedroom house in Pinner beforehand (my plan was to show Nathan an awful property first so that he would love the cottage as much as I did). We took a drive round Pinner, which is absolutely stunning, and then drove to the house. The street it was in was so quiet – all you could hear was the birds singing – and a man was out washing his car. I was starting to panic in case Nathan liked this house but fortunately it was truly awful inside!

We arrived about 30 mins early for the Moon Cottage viewing. Nathan was concerned about the busy road so we went to the White Bear to watch the traffic go past. I was quietly cursing every driver. Anyway, off we trotted to Shirley's and she invited us in as the estate agents were in the middle of a viewing. It couldn't have been better because we got to see what the cottage would look like when really lived in – and of course Shirley is just a beautiful person.

As soon as I walked in the front door I knew that I had been right and that I was willing to fight to the death for this place. By the time we had got to the kitchen Nathan was also smitten. He didn't say anything but I could just tell from his eyes. After Shirley had shown us all the hidden treasures in the cottage, we went to her place for a cup of tea. We stayed there for an hour and a half. I think I already told you that Nathan forgot he was in a different cottage and kept opening doors and cupboards in Shirley's home! Luckily Shirley didn't mind one bit. The visit just ended perfectly when we saw that she had a rabbit too.

Talking of which, as you know our rabbits are house rabbits and we haven't got any further with letting them outside yet, but that's the next step.

Move over cats, the rabbits are here!

With our warmest wishes,
Caroline

Dr Caroline Wallace
Science Policy Advisor

CHAPTER 13

John has come to stay with us for the night and, in the absence of a permanent parish priest at our local catholic church, he offers to say Mass the following day. The three of us leave early in the morning for Mass (making sure that the cats are firmly shut in) and afterwards I do some shopping, so I don't return to the Coach House until 11.30. Meanwhile, Michael and John have gone on to the local town of Kendal to pursue other matters. As I drive back to the Coach House the rain buckets down – it is positively tropical in its force. It is the sort of rain that if you are caught in it without an umbrella, every stitch of clothing is soaked within seconds of exposure and you can feel it running down your skin. I unlock the front door and walk in calling out to the cats. Pushkin and Fannie come to greet me and I assume that Titus and Gilly are asleep elsewhere. I go upstairs and suddenly I hear Gilly's unmistakeable voice full of outrage and protest, but from outside! As I rush to the front door, there she is, trying to get in, looking like a moth-eaten drowned rat. I am utterly confounded. How could she have got out? I let her in and towel her down. She has been out for the whole of the downpour, I reckon.

'It's nothing more than you deserve, young madam,' I joke with her as she complains at the rub-a-dub-scrub going on. I go up to my desk and start my day's work and, suddenly, from outside my study, from I think the bathroom, I hear an almighty crashing noise. I go out to see what is happening. Fannie is lying on the spare bed with an inscrutable expression on her face, but not looking disturbed – if anything looking rather pleased – so I have to assume Gilly is not in this room. Pushkin and Titus are both lying in my study on the chair together, but of Gilly there is no sign. I look everywhere: in the airing cupboard, the wardrobes and the boxes she routinely hides in, but there isn't a trace of her. As I go into the guest bathroom again, I see that John has left the window open about six inches, but I cannot believe she has got down from there. It is very high up. But the more I think about it, the more I am persuaded that she must have escaped that way, which also explains how she was out when I got back from the shopping. I go outside and call, but to no avail, so I let Fannie out in the hope that she will stir Gilly up. At this point John and Michael return, and John goes off in search of her and spots her way across the field at the back and eventually, with John in hot pursuit, she returns to the garden where I capture her and bring her in. We all go into the garden and look up at the bathroom window in amazement. There is a sloping drainpipe running down the side of the house just underneath the window and I suspect she must have tried to straddle that and fell off, hence the crash. I gulp, but she is fine and doesn't seem any the worse for wear. When she gets back into the house, as if proof were needed, she immediately leaps up onto the bathroom windowsill to try to repeat the performance, bashing her head forcefully against the now firmly closed window.

Talking of black magical things I have not yet envisaged Gilly as either a spider or a little black bear, but there is time for both of these incarnations. I receive this email from my agent in America, Melissa Chinchillo, who I have learned shares my love of cats. I beg her to send me information and pictures of her own cats after I discover that she gave a home to two feral cats from the 'wilds' of Staten Island – the picture of her cat LooLoo – a boy but he's cool with his name – wearing a pink feather boa is very special as you can see from Peter's drawing at the beginning of this chapter:

From: Melissa Chinchillo
To: Marilyn Edwards
Sent: Friday, May 06, 12:35 am
Subject: RE: The Cats on Hutton Roof

Dear Marilyn,

OK, I weaken. I am sending you a picture of my charming LooLoo (aka Buster, L'il Buddy, Rusty-Buster, Petey, and Sparkey). Not sure if I mentioned, but he's a male who was mistakenly thought to be female, so friends and family (particularly male ones) insist on giving him boyish nicknames. But I maintain that he is LooLoo through and through and is quite happy with his name and to wear fancy costumes. He dragged that poor pink boa around the apartment until I finally had to throw it away – and he loves all sorts of necklaces and bow ties. Go figure! He is the cat I so yearned for as a girl when I tortured my poor cats with dress-up.

Spydah (aka Spydey, L'il Biddy, and SweetPea) is quite camera-shy so I have none to show you at the moment. Spydah got her name because she's all black and was so wild when I first got her that she would scurry around like a little black spider. She has now become more like a graceful little black bear.

It was quite an experience bringing them home from the wilds of Staten Island (that's a bit of geographical joke; it's quite a populated place)! They hid in my bedroom behind and underneath furniture and would only come out at night when I was 'sleeping' (not with them in the room!) and tear around the room. I wasn't sure if they were playing or just very freaked out. I worried for a long time because it took about 3–4 months for them to finally be affectionate, though they began playing with me after 1 month. But they would run away if I ever tried to pet them . . . But it was a fantastic learning experience on how to gain their trust – especially after their first trip to the vet when we had a little progress, and it was dashed because they were so torn up by going in their carry-cages and being driven in a car . . . Now, you'd never know they were feral . . . except a little with Spydah, as she can sometimes be shy. She was the runt of the litter, the woman who gave them to me said, and she still has a little of that mentality compared to her huge brother. He sometimes horses around with her too much for her liking and then she'll take to under the bed.

I try at all costs to give Spydey lots of one-on-one

affection, separate from LooLoo, because he'll try to steal the show – and eat her food – at all costs. Right this moment, he's on my desk as I type and Spydah is patiently poised on my bed behind me waiting for me to give her a snuggle.

All the best,

Melissa

🐾 🐾 🐾

In early June France and Mark come up to see us, bringing with them the most wonderful drawing in crayons of Pushkin[15] that France has secretly drawn for me as a gift. I am astonished at the way she can capture the essence of a particular cat's personality and character. She is a talented artist. While they are here she takes a large number of pictures of the other cats, and later on I receive the most amazing portrait of Fannie, who has a special place in my heart as she knows. Over a long leisurely lunch France tells me about Spooky who has just had

---

[15] Both the pastels of Pushkin and of Fannie can be seen on my website under the names of the individual cats: www.thecatsofmooncottage.co.uk

kittens. The litter consists of just two – a tortoise-shell girl with a lot of white and a mainly black boy, with a small amount of white. Mother and kittens are all doing well.

The actual birth happened at an especially awkward moment for her as she was involved in giving a private French lesson in her house with two of the children from her school. Spooky absolutely insisted that France should leave everything and go upstairs to be with her. I am very touched that her queen depends upon France each time to act as midwife.

'We all sat on the floor so I could keep close to Spooky while trying to teach French at the same time. I had prepared her a nest at the right end of the wardrobe, but she would have none of it. This time she had decided she would have them in the left half of the wardrobe, over all the Christmas paper, bags, cards, other wrapping stuff and junk I keep there. So I had to empty it all (still trying to do my French lesson at the same time) and replace the bedding there. My lesson finished, the kids had to leave, and unfortunately for them, the first kitten was born only minutes after their departure.'

After France and Mark return back home to Spooky and her kittens (they had a neighbour cat-sitting while they were away), I get an update. The kittens have their eyes open at last. She has been quite concerned as kittens normally open their eyes between five and ten days of age, but Chester and Harriet, as these two kittens are called, didn't open theirs until they were twelve days old. She has just heard that they are to be adopted as a pair by her local butcher's wife, a lady called Kath, who plans to get a puppy at the same time. Kath lives locally, and this means that France will be able to see the kittens as often as she likes, which pleases her enormously. It also helps France to know that there is no point in allowing herself to feel broody, as she has the same weakness for kittens that I have. France gives me regular updates on their development over the next few weeks and then I get an email from her, explaining a particularly eventful party that she and Mark held over the weekend for assorted friends.

From: France Bauduin
To: Marilyn Edwards
Sent: July 11th 15:39

Well, so much happened yesterday, I had to write to give you an update on the kittens.

The kittens have now found out how to get downstairs. That, on its own, was a good new experience for them. But once people started arriving for our BBQ, they suddenly discovered a new kind of human too, the kind that runs, yells, and carries you all over the place like a rag doll: Kids!!! There were 4 little girls (5, 7, 8 and 13), the 5 year-old being a hyperactive kid at that. Chester took it all very well; he accepted being carried everywhere without batting an eyelid, as if it was mummy doing it. Harriet, though, became increasingly spooked and would try to hide whenever she could to avoid being handled.

Well, I couldn't be everywhere so just had to take it on trust that the kittens would be alright.

A couple of hours later, just as the BBQ, complete with oven BBQ chicken, sausages, burger steaks and salads, was about to be served, the little girl came to see me worriedly. They just couldn't find the kittens. At first, I was not too worried. Obviously, they had found some place to hide away and get a bit of peace. Except that when I came upstairs, I noticed someone had fully opened the window and this is one of the places the kittens can easily climb to. Good grief, had they fallen off the window? With the kids, I looked again in all the known hiding places they had used since they were born. I couldn't find them anywhere. I looked at other possible places. No kittens. I gave a quick look outside but couldn't see either of them. The only thing that was keeping me from utterly panicking was that Spooky was in our bedroom and didn't seem worried. If they had fallen through the window, surely she would have heard them and be looking for them.

Well, in the end, I found them. They were in my wardrobe, sleeping between my shoes under the shoe rack. Thank God for that! I could finally attend to my guests and have some supper myself.

The rest of the evening passed smoothly enough. Both Grippette and Uni came to say hello but legged it soon afterwards finding there was too much activity for their taste.

By the end of the evening, however, I heard Spooky's

worried calls: the ones she makes when she is looking for her kittens and can't find them. Someone had left the back door open, and both kittens were playing in the backyard in the dark. Talk about a day of discoveries, going from being penned upstairs to finding downstairs and the backyard all in one day. I got Harriet easily (being mostly white) but Chester was a little more difficult to spot (being almost all black). The little devils!

Today the back door remains closed as all the windows (well they are opened up 1 inch or so). Not great especially in this heat but I just don't want to have to worry. Yesterday was enough for the week.

Only 2 weeks to go before I give them away. Not long. At least I am on Holiday and can spare more time to play with them.

Love France.

I continue to get progress reports from France and shortly after this she tells me of an occasion when Spooky comes into the house carrying the largest dead mouse she has ever seen. Her account makes me laugh as it is clearly the all-important lesson that maternal cats give to their offspring at a certain stage in their development; it is exactly what Otto did when Fannie and Titus were only a few weeks old.

'When she saw me come to her, she put it down and just left it there. So right, I get the message. I am to bring the kittens to the mouse, I am after all their "auntie" and "kitten-sitter", so I must assume my responsibilities at all costs. This time the reaction was fantastic: proper kitten reactions at last. They fought for it, threw it in the air, and growled "MINE!" "MINE!" at each other.'

And so the kittens are growing up fast. France tells me that as the kittens get older, then Spooky's attitude towards them is changing, and she is much less protective towards them. At nine weeks old they are about to go for their first set of injections and she and Kath, who is soon to be their new human companion, both use the same vet which is useful. I know that France is dreading the moment of handover for herself and also for poor Spooky. She next contacts me as follows:

'For Spooky, she didn't seem to miss them too much in the evening but started miaowing and looking for them in the middle of the night, coming to lie on me three times to take some comfort from me. Spooky rarely does that. To do it three times in the same night shows how much she missed the kittens and was trying to find a bit of reassurance and love elsewhere. This morning she's been sleeping most of the time. Kath called this morning to give me an update on the kittens. She said they settled down very well, especially Chester who was very happy to flop on anyone's lap for a nap. Harriet seems very happy as well and they have been playing all morning.' France then confesses that she has felt the need to bike over to them and check them out for herself. She reports back that the kittens are fit and well and clearly being looked after supremely well in their new home. Spooky is still calling for them but less often and is on her way to recovery, ditto France I hope, but as displacement activity I suspect, I get this:

From: France Bauduin
To: Marilyn Edwards
Sent: July 30th 18:44

Here is a drawing I have done of Harriet and Chester together.

CHAPTER 14

The situation continues to be tense between Fannie and Gilly. I keep convincing myself that Gilly is only trying to play; sometimes when she sits and toughs it out with Fannie, Fannie does seem to be her own worst enemy. Fannie, on first seeing Gilly, will hiss whether there is any chase implicit or not, and as Gilly stares at her, Fannie always chooses a course of action which is doomed. She will half crouch, half lie on the ground, with her ears pinned back along her head, and hiss repeatedly, the hisses getting progressively louder. If she were ever to walk towards Gilly, as do Titus and Pushkin, then Gilly would back down, but she never does. Gilly will now creep closer and closer with her pricked ears quivering and her whiskers angled forward inquiringly as when a cat stalks prey, and as she gets closer, in the absence of retaliation the only action open to Fannie is for her to turn tail and run, at which point Gilly takes off after her in full pursuit. I comfort Fannie when this happens but realise there is a risk that it will encourage her to play the 'pathetic' card even more than she already does.

When Gilly tries the same tack, exactly, with Titus, Titus just thrashes her tail around violently and either stays still or walks slowly around the 'obstruction' of Gilly. With Pushkin, depending upon his mood, he either runs away or, now increasingly, he will half run away and then you can almost see him consciously change his mind when he stops abruptly, turns and chases Gilly, who in turn responds by running away. The cruellest thing of all now is that Pushkin has just taken to regularly chasing the woebegone Fannie, which is really harsh when all those months when she was on heat and calling to him, he would never go near her. He clearly doesn't chase her meaning to harm her, but she is so muddled up and disturbed by

Gilly that her reaction to him is exactly the same as her reaction to Gilly. You can tell from his body language after he has chased Fannie that he actually thinks it's rather a good wheeze.

All four cats have been going out more frequently and for longer spells and indeed we leave Titus out for as long as she wants, as she mainly goes into the field at the back and then comes back on her own. The only downside of Titus's spells outside is that she eats a lot of meadow grass and then promptly comes in to be sick. Why do cats come inside to be sick? Maybe it's a need for privacy as vomiting in the open air would highlight your vulnerability? Fannie spends less and less time outside at the moment; she can't cope with being chased by Gilly outside, although mainly Gilly ignores her when they are in the garden. Pushkin, on the other hand, who held top position until very recently as the most timid of the three cats, now spends more time out because, sadly, he caught a blackbird fledgling and is clearly on the lookout for more. Of all of them, though, Gilly is the loose cannon as she spends her time anywhere and everywhere running wildly at high speeds and without any care for where she is going, so it could as easily be the road as the field at the back. She runs round our garden, round Richard and Annabel's garden, in the road, anywhere she pleases, and I just pray. Michael has a theory that Fannie sends her out there on a daily basis.

Today I go to see my dear friend Brian, who lives over in Richmond at the eastern end of Swaledale. He is valiantly confronting recent widowhood and the aftermath of what he refers to as 'a dyno-rod job' on his prostate. While sitting on a rickety bench outside his house, glass in hand, Brian regales me, against the sound of tractor-drawn hay-wains thundering past, with a tale of how he and Valerie, setting out on a long research visit to New York, had arranged to stay with two old friends who had an extremely chic apartment on Roosevelt Island in the City's East River. Hospitality was always unstintingly offered, but Valerie used to recount how full residents' rights were only granted after she had been interviewed by no fewer than five cats who lined up on a sofa to inspect her and assure themselves that she would pass muster. (The trip proved a great success and the book that emerged from it was dedicated to 'Ray and Peter and the Famous Five' – although one of those five went some way towards derailing things near the start when Brian – last man out in the morning departure – failed to check the whereabouts of everyone and found, returning that evening, that the Cat Frederick had been shut in a bedroom with serious consequences visited upon a swan's-down duvet and he, Brian, now in receipt of a yellow card as a result.)

The following day Brian and I take a gentle walk with Jessie, his much-loved Cairn terrier, in the grounds of Easby Abbey. As we walk I am moved by the sense of complete quiet and tranquillity that emanates out of every block of stone of these ancient ruins, and its surrounding woodland, where the loudest sound is the soft coo-coo-cooing of a plump woodpigeon calling to its mate. The ruins of the Abbey lie alongside the River Swale and it was originally inhabited by Premonstratensian Canons known locally as the White Canons (because their habits were white). At the time Easby was built, there was also a Benedictine priory, St Martin's, a mile upstream on the other side of the river, whose monks wore black habits. The mind conjures up a delicious monochromatic image of these two groups of religious facing each other across the river like pieces from a living chess set. When I make this observation to Brian he chortles:

'A bit like "Alice" – but did you know that her progenitor was at school in Richmond before going to Rugby and would have known the valley and Easby and all!'

'Hey, you don't think that when he wrote . . . No, it would be too much of a coincidence?'

Quite why the Abbey feels as tranquil as it does I am not sure as it has had a fairly tortured existence. The White Canons, like the Benedictines, followed a simple and austere life, but they were in constant danger of being raided by the Scots and were obliged to call in the English army for protection. They got it, but at a fearful cost. In 1346, an English army, on its way to the Battle of Neville's Cross, was billeted in the Abbey. The soldiers spent most of the time in drunken brawling and inflicted as much damage on the Abbey as the Scots would have done. Eventually the Abbey suffered further looting and destruction with the Dissolution of the Monasteries and was finally abandoned;[16] a sad place, but all the same, breathtakingly beautiful.

After saying farewell to Brian and Jessie I drive back from Richmond taking the low road home which comes winding down through the thick woods beside the Swale and am enchanted by the slanting golden sunlight of this late spring/early summer and it melts my heart. The varied green of the leaves is almost throbbing in its intensity and the colour everywhere is violently bright. I have a sense of long shadows and golden light and as I drive through it I feel an ardent allegiance to it – this particular light, this precise lie of the land, could not be anywhere else. They are unique to this hemisphere, to this continent, to this island. This is where I belong.

---

[16] this historical information from *A look at Richmond* by John Ryder (Welbury Press) ISBN 0 905826 00 0.

🐦 🐦 🐦

Today is Midsummer's Day and today, Hugh, our great nephew comes to visit Michael and me for the first time. Hugh is the eleven-month-old son of Claire and grandson of Catherine, Michael's sister, and he was born shortly after our grandson Oskar, whom we both miss terribly because he lives far away in Sweden, so we are enchanted to get a baby-fix.

I am bewitched by the interaction between Hugh and Gilly. Gilly has never met a small child in her life before and is not at all sure how to take him, but Hugh is utterly trusting of Gilly, as he has a much-loved and loving cat at home with whom he plays happily for hours. Gilly watches him and soon he starts to crawl around the floor chasing her. She adores this but keeps running away from him – it is very funny to see the chaser being chased for once, but she keeps peeping out round the corners of her hiding places when she deems that his progress is too slow to make sure that he is still in pursuit. Over lunch Claire straps Hugh into his pushchair and Gilly, sitting above him on the cat platform, suddenly puts out her paw, claws fully retracted, I gratefully observe, and pats him lightly on the head, several times.

'I reckon she is trying to work out what exactly he is,' Michael observes. 'Is he fish, is he fowl, or is he good red herring? Oh silly Gilly, he is none of those things; he is just a human kitten, only younger even than you.'

As our lunch progresses Catherine entertains us with her tales of Baldrick, their fifteen-year-old ginger moggy who, rather like Titus, has always had difficulty in jumping and climbing and, when he feels the time has come to ascend onto their bed, spends several concentrated seconds swaying his backside from side to side in the manner of a sumo wrestler psyching himself up in order to make that effortful spring which will, in Baldrick's case he hopes, result in his landing four-square on top of the bed.

Dear old Baldrick who, when he first arrived in the

Hughes household having been named 'Baby' by the RSPCA as the smallest and scruffiest of several siblings who had temporarily been homed there following the death of their mother on the road, was greeted with enthusiasm by Ray, who announced:

'I have just the name for you, my boy. "Baldrick" it is from now on', and so it has remained. Baldrick, who at the age of eight weeks, was greeted by their long-resident queen, Nellie, with a hatred and irritation that she never wholly lost and which she manifested by removing a piece of Baldrick's ear, and it remains a notable battle scar to this day. Whether it was Nellie's personality or not it is hard to say, but while she lived Baldrick remained silent. However, following her death at the venerable age of twenty years, Baldrick has now taken on her role and has found his voice and noisily miaows his greetings and demands for food, which he would never have done while Nellie was around.

Since writing the above I have had the sad news from Catherine that Baldrick has rejoined Nellie, but one hopes, with his voice intact. Baldrick, please rest in peace.

CHAPTER 15

I confess it, a new love: the bumblebee! I am captivated by them and feel so guilty that I have never before understood why they are so wonderful. They, more than any other insect, have become for me the harbinger of spring. Although it is now midsummer I here record that from mid-March onwards our garden was host to many slow and lumbering bumblebees and I was alarmed for them as the frosts were not yet finished when first I saw them, although the days I did spot them early were always mild and sunny. I didn't then know why or what they were about, only that they were astonishingly early, until I came across a completely wonderful book which is now my bumble-bee bible.[17] From this book I learned that the early bees that I was seeing were all queen bumblebees, newly awakened from winter hibernation, having been fertilised by their chosen male in the autumn, and now desperately trying to replenish their lost body fats with pollen and nectar from suitable plants. The reason they seemed so slow is that they were just able to generate enough body heat to get off the ground, but only just. Their solemn and solitary task from late February until early May, depending upon the species, was first to feed up in order to develop their fertilised ovaries and then to find a suitable location for a nest to start the new colony. The bumblebees that I spied in those first spring days were probably the common *bombus terrestris*, although they are very similar in appearance to *bombus pratorum* who are also widespread early bumblebees, but I am sure that it was one or the other, and for both species

---

[17] *Field Guide to the Bumblebees of Great Britain & Ireland* by Mike Edwards and Martin Jenner (Ocelli, 2005) £9.99, ISBN 0954971302. Their argument for using only the scientific names is very persuasive.

their chosen nesting sites are in undergrowth or even underground. I discover from my bumblebee mentor and namesake (but sadly no relation) Mike Edwards that these feisty queens, having chosen their nest site, would have formed a ball of pollen within it and made a nectar pot and, surrounded by these home comforts, would then have set out about reproducing their first offspring, which would be worker bees, and these workers would all be *female*. Worker bees can only produce male bees themselves and, at this crucial early stage, the queen then 'instructs' them that they may not produce bees; they must go out and bring in food, and this they do, their function being to forage and care for the colony, although if death and destruction were to deprive them of their queen, without aid of fertilisation they could produce males.

In March and April our garden had many early flowering plants, some early heathers,[18] crocus,[19] cowslips,[20] rosemary,[21] flowering

---

[18] erica

[19] crocus

[20] primula

[21] rosmarinus

currant,[22]   rhodo-
dendrons,[23] clematis[24]
and gorse[25] I have also
just found my pressed
flower album and on
10 April, coming back
from church, Michael and
I picked from the hedgerow
just down the road some bluebells,[26]
primroses,[27] cowslips,[28] aconites[29] and blackthorn,[30]
all beloved by bumblebees, and there they are,
looking a bit squashed (and Gilly has eaten most of
the bluebell) but a true relic of our early spring.

This being nature, and red in tooth and claw, I
discover that there is a group of bumblebees called
cuckoo bumblebees who are parasitic on social

---

[22] ribes
[23] rhododendrons
[24] clematis
[25] ulex europaeus
[26] endymion
[27] primula veris
[28] primula
[29] aconitum
[30] prunus spinosa

bumblebees and in May the female cuckoo bumblebee, *bombus psithyrus*, who is large and powerful will usurp a social bumblebee's nest and will either 'hypnotise' (subdue her chemically) or kill the queen and take over the workers to care for her own offspring. For more information on true and fake bumblebees do seek out this wonderful tome. It is a great work of painstaking observation and says more about bumblebees than any other guide I have seen.

In late May and through June the bumblebees were unbridled in their desire for the nectar contained within the tight little whitey-pink flowers of the cotoneaster[31] that clambers rampantly up our gatepost and over our gate and also spills over the dividing wall from the Old Vicarage. However diminutive a flower it may bear, it seems to make no difference at all to the busy bumbling bumblebees, as it seems it's the all-important elixir contained within that must be sought out at all costs. I am intrigued by how bumblebees will visit the same flower again and again, supping only a

---

[31] corokia

little on each visit, as if in exacting obedience to some predetermined directive of 'little and often'.

The cats through this early summer are continuing to hone their hunting skills and Fannie catches and partially eats, with great flamboyance, two mice on consecutive days. Pushkin, although less successful than Fannie, spends long hours staring at one hole in the ground and presumably has in the past been successful using this technique, otherwise surely he would give up on it. Titus tends to just lie and twitch her tail and join in any other successful rounding up of prey that the others have engendered. Gilly, twice, rather sweetly brings in curled up brown leaves with great triumph, which she bats around, jumps on, holds aloft in her paws while lying on her back, exactly as if they were small mice and which, initially, fools the other cats who gather round expectantly but who then wander off, disdainfully, as they realise the whole thing is a complete humbug. This morning, however, it is a different story. Gilly catches her first mouse. It is alive and well and has no teeth marks on it, but it is very frightened. Michael and I gently remove it from her, and Michael takes it away into a field the other side of the road where she never goes, but after we remove it from her, she goes rigid with rage in my arms, like a two-year-old with temper tantrums, and in the end I have to put her down as I am fearful she will start biting and clawing. She so clearly understands the difference between the real thing and her former little brown leaves. Shortly after this, within just a few days, she catches and kills a blue tit, which I find her with in the sitting-room, tossing it around as if it were a toy, although the truth is, I suppose, that cats toss toys around as if they were dead birds. As before when the cats caught a blue tit, I am astonished that such a tiny bird has so many thousands of feathers. She then catches a greenfinch and after that a dunnock. I am beginning to be worried now. The bird kill has been comparatively low so far and part of the joy of living here is the wealth of birdlife, which I am anxious we do not unbalance. Gilly isn't very efficient at killing them, but just brilliant at catching them – she seems to have an instinctive sense of self and is skilful at concealing herself. She, like Pushkin, will sit it out for hours, but in Gilly's case she makes sure she is hidden under a bush, whereas Pushkin usually remains visible to all. Fannie continues to garner and kill shrews, field mice and field voles. Her greatest number of catches recently has been field voles, with their tiny round ears and short tails. It is said that a vole's innards taste bad to cats. Fannie eats part of them, the head usually, but leaves the rest, although she seems to eat all of the mice she captures, so perhaps this is true.

The hayfield behind the Coach House is growing higher by the day and nestling among the tall grasses is an abundance of wild flowers. Predominant among them is meadow buttercup,[32] but red clover[33] runs a close second followed by ribwort plantains.[34] Buried amidst this profusion and lower to the ground is the delicate bluey-violet of tufted vetch[35] and meadow crane's-bill[36] and today, walking carefully near the edge so that I don't flatten it, I find the wonderful tall yellow rattle or hay rattle,[37] and tradition dictates that when its seed pods rattle it's time to mow the hay, but at the moment it is still in glorious yellow flower. This hayfield is a wonderful species-rich meadow and looking out from the kitchen window over its butter-yellow, pink and blue flowers bobbing and dancing amongst the lush grasses makes me ache with pleasure. We find ourselves laughing every time we let Gilly out because when she finally squeezes herself through the fence and into the field at the back she unfailingly begins a series of enormous

---

[32] Ranunculus acris
[33] Trifolium pratense
[34] Plantago lanceolata
[35] Vicia cracca
[36] Geranium pratense
[37] Rhinanthus minor

springy jumps, which enable her to cover great distances over the meadow grass and the wild flowers. Unlike Gilly, with her energetic leapfrog-gings, all three of the older cats force their way through the long grass with apparent reluctance, and when it's been raining and there is a danger they might get wet they just turn tail and give up on it. And then, one dry and sunny day, the field is mown flat in preparation for a group of campers as the grass is now far too long for the comfortable pitching of a tent and it is dry and sunny at the moment, but rain is forecast. As we watch them lay low the grass and flowers with a powerful tractor and scythe attachment I am just a little afraid for the bumblebees that their vital supply of clover nectar has been cut short, as although much of the clover has died back there are still some healthy blossoms in there. But I need not have worried as, immediately the hay-meadow is flattened, the bumblebees appear to move en masse to the tiny bell-shaped pink flowers that almost invisibly (to us but not them) adorn the hedgerow on all the boundaries of the field, and completely surround our house. This thick hedgerow, so irresistibly attractive to bees, consists mainly of the dense shrub called snowberry[38] As I turn towards the house, the hedges are positively thrumming with the low buzzing of many tens of fat furry bumblebees and from time to time I spot a few of Richard's delicate slim honey bees balletically darting around their heavier distant-relatives, reminding me of a scene from my late childhood, when a gang of us girls, taking part in a gymkhana on our pint-sized ponies, caused disarray by mistakenly cantering into a field in which two sets of shire horses were performing a sample ploughing, to our chagrin and the mirth of the many onlookers.

As soon as the farmers leave the field, having baled and wrapped the silage, I let the cats out to see what they make of it. Fannie and Titus rush into the field with their tails up, clearly more at ease now that they have their old familiar long-distance view back, although Fannie stops short, suspiciously, as soon as she sees the big bale just outside the kitchen window. Gilly, on the other

---

[38] Symphoricarpos albus

hand, is agitated by the whole thing as her only memory seems to be of the tall grass which she liked and this new, long vista dotted with giant black bundles and its overpowering scent of mown hay is most worrying. She stands and sniffs repeatedly and then, perceptibly trembling, she quickly turns about and runs through the fence back into the garden. She is still only a little kitten at heart, for all her spirit.

It is now high summer and the weather for days on end has been sunny and beautiful – indeed, it is exceptionally dry for Cumbria. I have taken to writing out in the garden, under the shade of the giant Scots Pines, and both Gilly and Fannie come up to me from time to time to check that I am still at it, just as Michael does! I work at the big garden table and have a chair by the side of the one I am sitting on, which has a cushion on it. Fannie curls up on it proprietorially and writing at the table with her beside me in my domestic wilderness does properly make it 'Paradise enow'. Very quickly, however, I realise that this is going to mean trouble when I get checked out by Pushkin and Titus as well, who eye her keenly, so to avoid noses being put out of joint I surround myself with four chairs each with its cushion, just in case. Settling down to write outside is now a huge kerfuffle as I carry out the laptop, the extension lead, the dictionary, the chairs, the cushions, added to which periodically I have to move around to avoid the sun sneaking through the overhead branches and dazzling me. It is also entertainingly distracting, not least because I am concealed from the road, but can hear the ardent conversations and sometimes arguments of the hot sweaty walkers, having just climbed the hill from the village, as they innocently tramp past on their way up to the Crag. Life is hard! As I sit here I luxuriate in the mellifluous bird song coming at me from all angles and in particular that budgie-like chitter-chattering of swallows that is both extraordinarily comforting and at the same time exotic. Another prevalent exotic sound around here is the tinkling-bell call of the goldfinches.

Not all is peaceful, however. Gilly sometimes just goes too far in her assaults on Fannie and today she attacks Fannie in the guest bathroom, causing her to shriek with terror, although it isn't a real fight, Fannie is overreacting as usual. I am so cross that I tap Gilly on the nose, although I know full well that physical discipline and shouting is not the way to coerce cats into better behaviour, and say very sternly: 'Naughty, naughty cat' and push her outside the bathroom. She really glares at me as I do this. She turns away from me and I watch her flounce off downstairs. The whole way down she complains with her coarse baritone 'miaow, miaow, miaow' and I can hear her carrying on with it right through the conservatory and along into the other part of the house and up the stairs into our bedroom. My sense of remorse (she is after all only a very young cat still) makes me go and seek her out, after first comforting Fannie and settling her down in my study. When I reach Gilly she doesn't want to be cuddled and is very cross with me. We talk a bit about it all and although I don't believe she ends up thinking I was right in what I did, we part on better terms.

All that took place yesterday, but today she has a really bad fight with Fannie and Fannie is so jumpy that she just retires to her little box on top of the filing cabinet. Although Gilly has now usurped every other resting place that Fannie has hitherto slept in, this box, although she could get into it, she has left alone. I tremble for Fannie at the thought of what she or I will do when Gilly finally hijacks that one as well. Sometimes Fannie still gets up on top of the bookcase, but she feels less secure up there as Gilly often climbs up there too, although Gilly has fallen down at least twice while in the process of climbing up.

CHAPTER 16

The bird kill that I have witnessed through the summer is worrying me and although I have mixed feelings about cat collars, I did have one on my former cat Otto, complete with bell, and she killed, I believe, only one bird in her life. I study the RSPB website and find an article headed:

COLLAR THAT CAT TO SAVE
WILDLIFE!

A correctly fitted collar and bell can reduce cat predation by a third, according to new RSPB research. The study, undertaken by volunteer cat owners from across the UK, tested the effect of different collar-mounted warning devices in reducing cat predation within gardens. Results show that cats equipped with a bell returned 41 per cent fewer birds and 34 per cent fewer mammals than those with a plain collar. Those equipped with an electronic sonic device returned 51 per cent fewer birds and 38 per cent fewer mammals, compared with cats wearing a plain collar.

I decide I should try what the RSPB advises as this summer four birds have met their end who would not otherwise have done so without the benefit of the Coach House cats, not to mention numerous small mammals, perhaps ten in total, mainly shrews, a few mice and one or two voles. Gilly manages to force her collar open (it has the safety fastening that Claire Bessant recommends on the RSPB website) twice within half an hour of first wearing it, and it does reassure me that it is easy to open on the safety count, but perhaps just too easy? Pushkin is appalled at the invasion of his body and his hearing in this way and slinks away tinkling his bell loudly to some hiding place where a cat might sit and mope who has been subjected to this indignity. Titus sits and takes it like the cat she is, but looks up at me with an expression of dignified hurt on her face that I am doing this horrible thing to her. Fannie rushes away and manages to rip it off five times in the first hour of her wearing it. When I do put it back on her after the fifth time of her removal, she just looks at me with large eyes filled with fear and in front of me scratches the safety lock open within ten seconds with what I take to be a combination of iron will and pleading. At this point I capitulate as she is so stricken by her relationship with Gilly that I feel she just doesn't need more grief in her life at the moment. I find the other cats and it is clear that the tinkling bells (they are surprisingly loud) are causing them considerable stress, so one by one over a period of twenty-four hours I remove the bells, but leave the collars as I have now paid for engraved identity discs which will be coming shortly and need the collars from which to hang them. Through each of the subsequent two nights I wake at intervals to hear one or other of the cats scratching, scratching, scratching, but all three now keep the collars round their necks for all their efforts. I do need to find a different collar for Fannie, when the discs arrive, but am still worried about her reaction. I will wait to see whether the others get used to them.

Honourably, I will try to record all bird kill from now. I do realise that without bells to ward off the victims of their hunting sprees their collars are useless, other than to identify them if they get lost, but I would like to hope that their kill rate is sufficiently low not to merit the ding-a-ling harassment these bells would otherwise give them. The mind boggles at the effect the sonic devices must have on the sensitive hearing of cats. I am encouraged in my pursuit of a bell-less course when Sue Fallon, a new email friend and cat-lover, replies to my question on bells with:

— — —

From: Sue Fallon
To: Marilyn Edwards
Sent: Friday, July 29, 1:32 PM
Subject: RE: Bells

Hello Marilyn,

Cats and bells – my cats wear collars (apart from Syddy who always gets them in his mouth and gets the collar stuck in his teeth). I remove the bells, though, as I read many moons (excuse the pun) ago that cats have such sensitive hearing that even a little bell is like having a cow bell clanking in their head 24/7. If they are going to catch birds it seems that cats are clever enough to be able to stop the bell (I have observed this myself from the days when they did have bells). It is amazing that they can do it, but bells that have been tinkling away suddenly stop as they begin to stalk. On average I think my lot take about 4 or 5 birds between them the whole year and I have a lot of birds in my garden. The ones they manage to catch are either sick or, sadly, the youngest who have not realised you're supposed to take off rapidly when a cat is spied. I even have a Robin who quite happily bobs around close to me while I am gardening and we have a meaningful conversation. (Did I mention that I was quite mad?). Obviously your cats are enjoying their new-found freedom?

Best wishes,

Sue

Sue is pretty good on cats. She has a remarkable nine, every one of which she adores. The oldest is Muffin at eleven, followed by Whatsit at seven, and mother of Syddy, Tymmy, Dympy and Mischief, all aged six, and the others are the brood of another – sadly missing – cat, who Sue continues to hope will one day come home, also six years old, and they are Butty, Jiffy and Flash.

One of Gilly's most appealing party tricks since her very first introduction into the Coach House has been to retrieve a small furry dark-blue bird on an elastic string (which lost its plastic eyes within the first five minutes of meeting Gilly). She will not 'fetch' any other toy, but if I sit on the sofa in the sitting-room and throw it into the kitchen she will race off, pick it up in her mouth and return, dropping it at my feet as if she were a small black Labrador. It provides me with endless fun, although when she was much younger she would gallop off to bring it back in what seemed then a tireless pursuit of it. Now in her older age (all of nine months) she sometimes rather arrogantly strolls off after it and, if she is really bored, just looks at me and drops it down again in the kitchen. I thought this was unique, but then I got this email from Suzanne and realised I was one of thousands who are bewitched by the talents of Bengals:

– – –

From: Suzanne
To: Marilyn
Sent: Thursday, July 14, 9:15 PM

Wait until my mum hears that you have a Bengal! She will be thrilled! Let me tell you, they are hard work. Cute as a button when they are kittens, but as they get older they turn into children! My dad isn't the biggest fan of cats. We've had so many over the years, and with these two around it drives him crazy! They literally run the household. They have such strong personalities. I think that is a Bengal's nature. I could tell you a million funny stories about the two of them . . . but the best one of all is how much they are like dogs! Seriously! Our youngest one, Luca, plays fetch! We didn't even have to teach him. He has a little green mouse that he plays with and one day we threw it for him and he brought it back. And he will do it over and over again until it drives you insane! He will only do it with that particular green mouse, strange.

So there you go! Gilly is just a clone of every other Bengal. No, of course she isn't, but there are clearly traits in Bengals that are specially theirs. (Since writing the above, two different cat-lovers who do not have Bengals have told me their cats retrieve, so I withdraw the statement that this is peculiar to Bengals!)

The relationship between Gilly and Fannie continues as uncomfortably as ever and I worry, as Fannie now seems to spend her entire time in my study or outside, but certainly doesn't seem able to live with us in the rest of the house. On the rare occasions now that she and I do share a cuddle in the morning after the bath, I actively have to seek her out and bring her into the bathroom and shut the door, so she can be assured that Gilly will not disrupt it. What on earth is going to happen in the winter and once the rains start in earnest and she cannot escape into the garden and the surrounding fields? Gilly is, however, an enchanting cat to have around the place, and both Michael and I adore her being part of our household and just long for the relationship between her and Fannie not to escalate to any more of a problem than it currently is. Michael continues to call her his 'Black Magic' and he is utterly besotted by her. Talking of which, Bengals of course, I receive an email from Beth, Treacle's carer and companion, who tells me that her move to more northern Scotland (she currently lives in an exquisite but remote part of the county of Dumfries and Galloway which is just reachable by us, but any further north and we are talking real cross-country journeying) is imminent and I realise that if I am to see Gilly's half-brother before he becomes inaccessible, then it is now or never. She adds the following at the end of her email:

From: Beth
To: Marilyn
Sent: Wednesday, August 03, 10:52

A blog entry

Yesterday, young Treacle went out at tea-time. It was a grey and miserable day, with a heavy drizzle. Shortly after tea, we realised that (a) Treacle wasn't around and (b) it was raining heavily. Mr L went to look for the cat; he wasn't at any of his usual entry stations, but could be heard crying pitifully. Mr L braved the storm and went outside to look, saying, 'Treacle is distressed' as he went out of the door. I was hunting for my shoes when I heard Ted shout. Two single cries, both the same. A very loud and harsh cry – 'OW!' I read it as a Bengal language version of 'Don't worry – I'll get you!' SuperTed flew out of the front door, metaphoric cape streaming in the wind created by his rushing. He stopped outside the porch. His head whipped first to the left, then just as quickly to the right. No Treacle! Then he looked up. RAIN!! – and indoors he bolted. What a wuss! Treacle was hiding under the veranda – and would not come out. Oh no – it's wet out there!

Cajoling him would bring him forward to the edge of the decking, but as soon as he saw the big drips, he backed up again. I lay on the floor, getting soaking wet and muddy. He just looked at me with those huge yellow eyes, and mewled an anguished 'I'm wet!'

It was Mr L's long arm that reached in and pulled the cat out. He was quickly popped back through the kitchen window and ran into the sitting room to be with his mate. A bone-dry Teddy, cool as a cucumber, offered up his services to help dry Treacle off, with a smug look on his face that said, 'See? I told you I would come and get you!' No matter how bad things get, the cats can always make us smile.

Beth

Beth commands a wonderful blog on her website about all manner of things, which often includes great stories about her cats, and it's well worth a visit by any cat lover. This is how you find her: http://www.woolgathering.org.uk. So without more ado Michael, John and I set off to the very tip of Dumfries and Galloway. Because I want to talk black cat with Beth and meet Treacle, I leave the men in a nearby small country town, to watch one of the first football matches of the season and, waving them merrily goodbye, I drive off into the Lowther hills. Treacle sure has got an idyllic place to hang out and lots of sheep to play with. Following Beth's immaculate driving instructions I finally find the village of Wanlockhead which, it proudly proclaims on a boundary board, is Scotland's highest village at 1,531 feet above sea level. That is high. I arrive at their house and am warmly welcomed by Griff, a very friendly mongrel collie, and Suzie, a Border collie, and Steve and Beth, and as we walk into their house, there I spy the illustrious Treacle. He is an astonishingly handsome cat. He has Gilly's looks but is more masculine and definite somehow. His blackness is as impenetrable as Gilly's and his silky-soft Bengal coat glistens as it catches the sunlight. As he turns side on I am able to admire his strong masculine profile. He swings back and stares steadily across at me with his penetrating yellow eyes. I very briefly meet Treacle's beloved feline companion, Teddy, a stunning brown marbled Bengal, but he hates me and my camera and runs away. I sadly never catch a glimpse of Lulu, Beth's Bengal cross, but she had warned me that Lulu was a complete recluse. Where they live is paradise, so where they are going to must be quite extraordinary. But after we talk for a bit I feel I really ought to let her get on with her dreaded packing, so I take my leave and drive off to find the boys.

Just before the close of August I hear, to my great pleasure, from Christopher Gordon, the brother of my dear deceased friend, Giles.

— — —

From: Christopher Gordon
To: Marilyn Edwards
Sent: Monday, August 22, 6:23 PM
Subject: Contact

Dear Marilyn
I will get back to you shortly about George, and I write with Cleo (sexy grey half-Burmese moggy) sitting on my desk and purring loudly. Somewhere I remember reading that Cardinal Richelieu usually had a cat on his desk when working, although I have to say I find it too distracting.

  Best wishes,
  Christopher

From: Marilyn Edwards
To: Christopher Gordon
Sent: Tuesday, August 23, 4:35
Subject: Re: contact

. . . PS Oh and do send my best to Cleo, and I am intrigued by what element in her you find sexy. You men(!) – Michael said something similar to me the other day about our black Bengal kitten (born around Halloween last year – she is a girl so we couldn't call her Giles – but we have called her Gilly in honour of your bro). She is sleek and slim and long legged and, as he was watching her sashaying towards the gate, he said, 'Oh, she is such a girl, she is so feminine' and there was a real yearning in his voice for her girlishness, it made me laugh.

   Marilyn

From: Christopher Gordon
To: Marilyn Edwards
Sent: Tuesday, August 23, 6:11 PM
Subject: Re: contact

We all clearly have a need for displacement activity!

August is not a great month in which to try and work . . .

What is so sexy about Cleo? Hmmm. . . being Cleo. I have a deeply unscientific theory that cats predominantly embody the female principle, dogs the male. Which is why I don't much care for dogs, I suspect. I mean, who wants to waste time or affection on a permanently attention-seeking animal with extrovert arrested teenage mentality, desperate for constant reassurance that it is loved? Ugh! It's demeaning, embarrassing and irksome – with the possible exception of collies. Dogs are just so boringly uncomplicated and predictable! The cat's introverted feminine self-sufficiency and moodiness, its need to be wooed, on the other hand . . . Was it something I did? No response. Was it something I said? No response. Was it something I didn't say? No response. Was it something you think I might have thought, that could have hurt your feelings if I'd ever got round to putting it into words? Maybe . . . Ah.

No, no, I never stereotype. I think that the combination of those cat eyes in an intelligent haughty face with its slightly smug self-contained expression is a big factor. It's a constant challenge. Cats flirt outrageously and tend to play hard to get. And when they don't, but flop down on the ground on their backs just for you, well, how can one resist? Dogs don't even know what flirting is. Not all cats are sexy. George isn't, although he has quite a sweet face, but it's just not very intelligent (but Cassandra, his black and white Persian predecessor, was). Cleo's predecessor – also grey Burmese – Scipio was dead sexy. He was very much a boy, and had those long legs (whereas Cleo, to be frank, having failed to do her post-natal exercises is now somewhat low slung). Dogs smell – although their owners always seem to deny this. Of course, cats don't. Though that reminds me people sometimes comment (with alarm!) on a habit I have of sniffing cat's paws as they lie in the sun – the combination of slightly warm sweaty pads/tufted fur is 100% redolent of being in a mosque in Istanbul – well, OK, I suppose it does come over as slightly weird. Whatever turns you on.

But enough of this – all the best,

Christopher

And following that Christopher then sends me this wonderful story about George, his cat, properly called George Pompidou, not because of any statesmanlike behaviour he manifested but because 'as a kitten he looked rather like a pompom'. Here is George's story as told by Christopher:

George is a black – with white paws, nose and bib – Persian moggie. He is not very bright. His life has always consisted mainly of sleeping outside in the sun, with two daily visits to the house for food (which you can set your clocks by – 7.30 a.m. and 5.00 p.m.). Despite being such an 'outdoor' cat, he is a completely hopeless hunter. Since his emergence from kittenhood, I can't recall him ever having moved faster than a slow stroll. He never threatens anything. Once when he was quite young and we lived in the Meon Valley, he did manage to catch a baby rabbit in a neighbouring field. Alex, our eldest boy (who has always had a sort of empathy with George, because this cat's rather pathetic nature amuses him), saw it happen. George miaowed – although the noise he makes is not impressive at the best of times – to draw attention to his prowess with the rabbit between his front paws and looked sideways to seek approval from Alex on the road. The rabbit escaped and hopped off – and George ignominiously failed to catch it again despite trying really hard. Nowadays in our more urban location in Winchester he

doesn't even bother to try. He sits on the grass surrounded by pigeons and blackbirds, which feed
contentedly only inches away from his nose. This can,
however, be misleading for the odd pigeon which
deduces a false syllogism: George is a wimp, George is
a cat, and therefore all cats are wimps. Other black and
white cats in our neighbourhood now take advantage of
the pigeons' thinking they are not a threat – so pigeons
must have even smaller brains than George.

Typically, the one 'event' in George's laid-back life
wasn't really an event at all. The location was the village
of Meonstoke where we then lived – or more accurately
Meonstoke and Corhampton, the adjoining village which
straddles the A32 road. It was in the middle of a hot
summer spell. Sue had just collected Adam, our fourth
and youngest child, from school during the afternoon
when she received a phone call to say that someone had
reported a dead cat lying on the side of the bend on the
A32 road near the village shop. It was a black and white
Persian, and it sounded very like George. Sue and Adam
duly went off to the scene of the accident, with Sue
doing her best to protect Adam from seeing the result of
the horrors of a head-on collision between a cat and a
passing vehicle. The face was, indeed, a complete mess

– but the small black spot on the predominantly white rear left leg clearly identified the corpse as George's.

They quickly returned home to seek out a winding sheet and box for the corpse, and then the two of them, with considerable effort, dug a grave in the hard soil at the bottom of the garden, alongside the final resting place of Chloe – another beloved family cat – who also came to grief on the road. The funeral service over, Sue and Adam returned to the house, where the latter began to inscribe a piece of slate with a suitable inscription to mark George's tomb. It was now 5.00 p.m. That hour that George never missed and sure enough George sauntered in demanding his tea . . . Never, until that moment, claims Sue, had she literally known what it meant for the jaw to drop. By a process of elimination we think we identified the true owner of the dead moggie in Corhampton, but the woman – who was not even in the habit of feeding her cats properly or regularly – denied it, so we will never know for sure who the cat who lies next to Chloe is.

Since telling the tale above of the Resurrection of George, just as this book is going to press, I receive the following email from Christopher:

– – –

From: Christopher Gordon
To: Marilyn Edwards
Sent: Thursday, March 02, 5:30 pm
Subject: End of story

Marilyn:

Just for the record, this is to report that George(s) (Pompidou) failed to appear for his food on Sunday last, and his body was found today in a shrubbery by one of our neighbours.

We'd been searching around and asking people in the locality over the past two or three days to check sheds etc., in case he had been shut in when they were working in their gardens on Saturday/Sunday.

He was 15 + and seems simply to have expired.

With best wishes,

Christopher

CHAPTER 17

It is now the end of the first week in August and it has been very dry for several weeks, and since the introduction of the collars on the cats at the end of July the scratching has continued. Gilly has stopped removing her collar, but oddly enough Titus, who had not mastered the art of escape at the beginning of the collar regime, now removes it every night, but rather artlessly leaves it on the end of our bed, so of course I replace it each morning. Michael is fondling Titus – minus collar – in bed early one morning when out of the silence he suddenly declares loudly:

'Marilyn, Titus has nasty lumps all round her neck.'

'Mnn – I know,' I mumble, trying desperately hard to hang on to that exquisite state of unconsciousness known to those not suffering from insomnia as 'sleep'.

'But they're really nasty. They have blood round them.' I rouse myself and have a look and rather than just scratching marks they do indeed possess the qualities of angry and painful lesions. Later on that morning I have another look and decide I must take her down to the long-suffering Gerard. I inspect all the other cats minutely. Fannie has a couple of small lumps but not angry and she hasn't been scratching, so she gets the all clear for the moment. I look all over Gilly and cannot see anything, so I reckon she is fine too. I find Pushkin asleep on the pillow on the spare bed and I gently remove his collar. To my concern he too has lumps where the collar had been, two or three and, although they are not livid, when I gently put pressure on them they are clearly irritating to him. I bundle him up in a cat cage and then go in search of Titus. Pushkin makes his petrified and unhappy girlish mewls. They are surprisingly falsetto and are getting higher and louder and under other circumstances they make me giggle, but today I am empathising with him and so they make me sweat slightly. I find and squash Titus into the smaller cat cage, which should properly have been Pushkin's, and she makes one protesting miaow and then falls silent. As I drive off with them together I realise that yet again poor Titus is being accompanied whether she likes it or not by the omnipresent Pushkin. When I arrive at the vet's and haul them out, I hear another feline patient's carer say, above a loud protesting racket coming from a carrying box:

'Can I just go out and get some rubber gloves, as I think he may bite and scratch when we get him out?' Ah, the joys of being a vet! We are called in and Gerard looks at Titus first. I am convinced that it must be the collars that are causing it, or possibly Titus is now allergic to the Metacam I give her for her arthritic legs from her earlier operations, and I baldly announce this. Gerard smiles at me benignly and lets me carry on and then, after carefully examining Titus and especially the area round her neck, he says quietly:

'Marilyn, this looks to me like a typical reaction

to harvest mite.[39] It is the larval stage that does the damage – they are almost invisible to the human eye, but they swarm up the cats from long grasses in late summer and early autumn and typically they get in between the toes. I was bitten myself on my back this weekend and it itches like mad.' He carefully studies both Titus and then Pushkin in minute detail and shows me exactly where they are irritated. I can see that the collars in themselves didn't cause the lesions, but rather the heat generated by the collars on the cats and the fact that their fur is thinner in that area was responsible for the attacks around their necks. I had noticed the cats attacking their feet too and this is more of the same. Apparently upland areas are especially prone to infestations of harvest mite, who love chalk and limestone and who proliferate in hot dry summers, and this has been unusually dry for Cumbria with its normal annual rainfall of between 60 and 100 inches. The larvae sneakily wait in large numbers on long grasses until a passing cat (apparently preferred) or human (next

---

[39] Trombicula autumnalis

best) comes into their zone, when they swarm over them and feast off their tissue fluid for three or four days before dropping off again on some other patch of grass to complete the rest of their life-cycle and to go on to produce more lovely harvest mites for next year. The cats are so irritated by the result of these infestations that Gerard decides he must inject them with a corticosteroid, but we both agree that if their reaction continues to be bad we need to find some other way of treating the problem.

Meanwhile I have a small project bubbling under, which in the way of small projects is turning in my mind into something more major. Michael and I have talked on and off about my keeping donkeys. I long for a little affectionate long-eared donkey, but the paddock we have across the road simply

 isn't big enough and, anyway, I know that if I had a donkey I would want two as company for each other. There is the small problem of

who might be persuaded to rent which field to us as almost all the fields are used year-round by sheep farmers who either own them or rent them from other farmers. On top of this the donkeys would need to be provided with proper shelter and I have talked in rather vague terms to Richard and Annabel and also to Ian in the village, but I keep stumbling upon various forms of resistance and I can feel my resolution breaking down. I did mention to Annabel that I might keep hens instead, as I used to keep hens when I lived in the Dales. Not the same thing at all as donkeys, I know, but they do at least have a practical purpose: one can eat their eggs. Annabel is rather keen on the idea which possibly means I could ask her to lock them up if we are away or out late which would make it workable: it is during the winter that keeping free-range poultry becomes most difficult. I now have the problem of persuading Michael.

'But what *is* the point of having hens? I simply don't get it.'

'They're hugely rewarding, they're funny and they're the only pets I know where you can eat their output.'

'But I can buy eggs, free-range eggs, from Anne down the road anytime we want them, you know that!'

'Yes, that's true, but I want the pleasure of watching hens and talking to them and being with them and, oh, just having them about the place. It is an amazingly tranquil and lovely thing to hear their little clucks and so good when you hear that triumphant chortle of "I've laid an egg! I've laid an egg! I've laid an egg!" and you would so love going to collect the eggs in the morning, you know you would, and anyway we need to do something with that weed-ridden paddock.'

'Marilyn, you told me you were either going to make it into a wild-flower meadow or a herb garden and you have had over a year to do it.'

'Oh I know, but go on I have made one bed into a herb garden already, and I've cleared a load of weeds away . . .' As I trail off, Michael clears his throat in a theatrical manner, so I gird my loins and continue:

'I'm not just making excuses, honestly, but the more I read about wild-flower meadows, the more I understand that it is a sort of battle and that usually the deep-rooted indigenous weeds triumph over everything else,' and more in that vein until our exchange fizzles out and the dust gently settles again.

Annabel, however, heroically comes to the rescue. Every time she meets Michael she bravely urges him to consider the efficacy and pleasures of hen husbandry and slowly I watch him yield. I realise only now how really very alarmed she must have been at the donkey idea, and it is true that some donkeys can disturb the peace mightily. I go down to see Anne at the Post Office to confess that I might be about to embark on the poultry route – Anne has a colourful collection of hens and bantams consisting of several breeds including Rhode Islands and Marans and she sells the eggs, so I am anxious to allay any fears she might have that I am setting up in competition. In the course of explaining where my hen-lust has sprung from, I tell her that I had really wanted donkeys and she tells me a wonderful story about a local farmer who used to give a group of donkeys from Morecambe Bay a winter break in a local field and that they regularly used to go into full unending bouts of braying that were enough to awaken the dead. However, their holidays in this part of the Lune valley ended when it was discovered that either in order to procure themselves a view of the crag or for the sheer hell of doing it or even I suppose inspired by their bellies, they had collectively eaten an enormous hole in the hedge. After that particular winter the Morecambe Bay donkeys were never to be seen in the village again.

For the last three Sundays John has been staying with us as he has been acting as supply priest to the catholic church in Kirkby Lonsdale in the interregnum between Fr John Turner leaving and the new priest, Fr Luiz Ruscillo, who is to take over some time in early September. Today John and Michael attack the little paddock in a way that I confess I had not managed on my own and, within a short space of time, the wildest of the weeds and their plastic carpets, which had been laid down by Pamela when she was operating her plant nursery, have been stripped out and the paddock reveals wonderful dark fallow soil just waiting for my wildflower meadow seeds to be sown. As the men collapse in exhaustion back in the garden of the

Coach House I eagerly go into battle with hoe and fork and start to prepare the seed bed. (John, who for many years was a priest in Zaire, comments that that is exactly how it is out there, the men do the heavy labouring on the land and then the women move in afterwards to sow the crops.) My meadow grass consists of various grasses including chewing's fescue, sheep's fescue, hard fescue, slender red fescue and crested dogtail, but alongside these grasses is a separate bag containing a glorious litany of wild flowers. Included are lady's bedstraw, ox-eye daisy, ribwort plantain, yarrow, wild carrot, self heal, red campion, viper's buglos, St John's wort, musk mallow, yellow rattle, meadow buttercup, primrose, B. knapweed, cowslip, rough hawkbit, ragged robin, and then additionally there is corn flower, corn chamomile, corn marigold, field poppy and black medick.

So after some toiling on my part, during which I exude a convincing display of sweat blood and tears (of effort), I finally get my seeds sown and join the boys over a bottle of wine to celebrate 'a job well done'.

'So all we have to do is sit back and wait for this

wonderful wild flower meadow to just spring up, is that it?' Michael teases me.

'Well, I reckon if the weather stays as it is – warm and alternately dry and wet in the right quantity, there is a good chance of it growing before winter . . . well, the grasses will and the flowers should come later.'

We talk for a while about the different breeds of hens and I explain to John and Michael why I'm especially keen to acquire pure Marans. I have always loved the so-called utility breeds of hen and for the size of eggs prefer larger hens rather than the little bantams which are great fun but tend to be rather flighty. But Marans, with their smart dark cuckoo colouring, are especially appealing as they lay the darkest brown eggs in the world.

'So when exactly are you thinking of getting these hens?'

'Oh, as soon as possible, but I have tried various sources on the internet, and pure Marans are hard to get, especially at this time of year, so I'm beginning to get a bit worried.'

'Oh, I know you, once you're on a "project" like this, there'll be no stopping you, I am sure you will find your hens before the autumn is out' and, sure enough, with the help of the Poultry Club of Great Britain and an exceptionally helpful hen breeder called Edward Boothman, I am finally directed to a master Maran breeder called Maurice Jackson, from whom I am able to reserve my point of lay pullets.

The cats continue to be troubled by the ubiquitous harvest mites and Pushkin attacks his feet regularly. Titus scratches periodically but not obsessively, and Fannie seems to be least afflicted, although from time to time I have seen her delicately chewing between her toes. Poor Gilly is the one, however, who seems to be suffering most. She has the most beautiful silky glossy fur and whether it is the quality of her fur that makes her skin so sensitive, who knows, but she licks compulsively and recently has taken to nibbling out the fur from her back legs, a little from her front legs and now her stomach, so she is rapidly assuming the mantle of one very moth-eaten cat who seems to be trying very hard to climb out of her fur. I take her back to Gerard, again, and he presents to us an elixir in an aerosol which contains a concentrate of Evening Primrose Oil which he hopes will help to encourage regrowth of her fur and perhaps help her itchiness.

'I rather think that Gilly has a very low threshold of itch,' he laughs and adds: 'I'm afraid this is what happens when you live in what appears to be the world's epicentre for the dreaded harvest mite.'

'I know, it's really terrible up in Hutton Roof and Michael is covered in bites all over his torso and his legs. It's funny but I never remember the estate agent mentioning this as a possible reason for not buying.'

'Yes, most unreasonable. You feel they should say something along the lines of "idyllic surroundings but completely uninhabitable between the months of August and November", do you?' he ribs me. I subsequently discover, though, that at least two of the women in the village cover themselves with Autan-Active insect repellent spray all day every day and again at night through the summer and autumn months to ward off the little devils. Next year, I promise myself, we will use the Autan and I will spray Frontline all over the cats before the mite cycle starts, which means beginning in July.

Pushkin has recently started a very bad thing when we let him out in the garden. He is now jumping on to the gate and running into Richard and Annabel's garden next door, and I have invited them both to shout at him forcefully to discourage these visits. Worst of all, Gilly, who greatly admires Pushkin and watches him closely, has found her own way into their garden also and is less intimidated by loud shouts.

Unconnected with the harvest mites, I think, I cannot fail to be aware of how the cats have yet again had a strange shake-up about where they are lying. I have noticed in the past that places that are their habitual resting places for months on end will suddenly go completely out of favour. Titus, for example, now spends most of her time sleeping on the landing at the top of the stairs, which is dark and draughty and hard. Pushkin sleeps on the floor in the spare bedroom which is almost as bad a place as the one chosen by Titus, and Fannie just stays up in her laundry box on top of the filing cabinet. Gilly sleeps mainly these days back on her igloo from her first home, which is in a box in my study.

On 5 September Maurice Jackson, his lovely smiley wife Ruth and a couple of their friends come over to the Coach House to deliver the eagerly awaited six Maran pullets which are now sixteen weeks old. They won't in fact lay until around twenty-three or twenty-four weeks, Maurice warns me. I am ridiculously excited. It is wonderful to take delivery of them. I have prepared for weeks, although the grass in the extended paddock is still growing and needs to be fully enclosed with chicken wire, so the first few weeks of their existence they will stay in the outer bit with access to the covered tunnel. A farming family in the village, the Armisteads, have very kindly sold to me for a very reasonable price two old-fashioned chicken coops, complete with slatted floors and sliding pop-hole doors that are around fifty years old and have been stored safely undercover for many a year and also an aluminium food storage container, and my old mate from the Dales, Thomas Raw, who helped me all those years ago with my Rhode Island Reds, comes over to help me again in adapting the coop with a perch and nest boxes. Wonderfully, he has never thrown away the original round-edged perches, the buckets, the water container, the dustbins for feed and my precious milk churn in which I stored the corn. Thank goodness for farmers and their hoarding instincts say I.

Maurice and I together unload the precious cargo, and as we carefully transfer each of the pullets from the two cat carriers that have acted as their means of transport into the hen coop, Maurice, who clearly knows everything there is to know about hens, suggests that I keep them penned up in their coop until 6 p.m. in the evening, then let them out and by 8 p.m. it will be near enough dusk for them to want to go back in to roost. Michael and I do that, but Michael is very uncertain about the whole thing.

'What on earth are you going to do when it gets dark, and you can't catch them?'

'Maurice swears it'll be alright, so I'm sure it will.' And sure enough, come dusk, at 7.50 p.m. exactly, they all walk back into the coop that they had been shut up in for most of the day and, when we lift the side lid, there they all are, neatly roosting up on the perch in a little line, except that Michael holds the lid open too long and two of them jump out again, but eventually it is fine and we all settle down for the night.

The following day we let them out and watch them with all the pride of newly adoptive parents. They are so cute and very curious. Their combs and wattles are still very small and pink rather than red, so they have a bit of growing to do yet awhile. In our time-honoured tradition of naming cats in a literary manner, we have decided to call the hens after women writers, all but one that is, who is called Alex, because Alex asked us to as she can no longer have a kitten. She will just have to write a book that is all. So they are, alphabetically, Agatha,

Alex, Charlotte, Emily, George and Jane. Agatha was the name that Michael chose and from this time on, whenever he praises any hen, he always calls her Agatha, regardless of whoever it is.

Shortly after this, although I have every confidence in my fescue meadow grasses, I worry about one non-productive part of the paddock and whether the hens will have enough grass, so with the much-appreciated help of Anthony Chaplow and his feisty two-year-old daughter Josie, from down in the village, turfs are neatly laid on the slow-growing section so that the hens will definitely have some fully developed grass before winter sets in.

The one dark shadow that hangs over us in all of this is that between the date I phoned Maurice and reserved my Maran hens and the hens arriving, worrying outbreaks of Avian flu have occurred in China and some gloom-mongers are saying it is bound to come across the whole of Europe and all free-range poultry will ultimately have to be culled.

CHAPTER 18

The phone goes early one evening as I am sitting at my desk staring at the computer screen. Stretching across to answer it, I look up out of the window and register dark storm clouds rolling down over the hills and see the branches blowing in the wind. It is the end of the first week in September and England has been enjoying a late summer heat wave, but the weather has turned suddenly and it's now distinctly autumnal. As I cradle the receiver to my ear I hear Michael speaking – uncharacter-istically quietly – and over his voice I can hear the sound of a woman sobbing. As I listen, my stomach contracts. There is a particular form of weeping that is unique to the newly bereaved that is distinct from all other forms of sorrow and I know this is what I am hearing.

'Mo, I am in the village. Little Oliver, the black kitten, is dead.' The sound of the adjacent sobs intensifies. Michael continues in a low voice:

'I am here helping Peter dig a grave, I am with Hilary. He was run over.' I gasp in horror and then ask:

'Michael, you weren't involved?'

'Of course not,' he remonstrates.

I feel wretched for the poor little cat who was so adorable and utterly desolated for the family who loved him so much.

'Should I come down?'

'Yes!'

I start to run down the hill and then, getting a stitch, have to slow down to a walk. I can feel tears dribbling down my face and am ashamed as what I feel must be as nothing compared with what the family who love him feel. That little black cat was the cutest cat in the world. He was special over and above the way that all cats – particularly loved cats – are special. He engendered affection in all who met him. He was extrovert, affectionate, purrful and a talented footballer to boot with a love of corks – when first I saw him I reckoned he was a Georgie or a Becks of a cat and then I teased Peter Warner that he may even have been a reincarnation of his beloved black cat Pelé and at one time he so nearly came to live with us.

As I approach Hilary and Phil's house I can see the outlined figures of Michael and Peter in the back garden digging with rugged determination and two young female figures standing close by with heads bowed down, who I realise must be Peter's sisters, Elizabeth and Catherine. I walk round the back of their house and there, in the middle of the lawn, is the forlorn figure of their once beautiful cat lying stretched out on a towel, bedraggled from the rain and stiff in death, and Hilary is kneeling on the grass next to him, crying quietly. The girls look utterly broken-hearted and Peter and Michael just keep their heads down and dig, dig, dig. Phil, their father, is still travelling home from work but Peter has phoned him to forewarn him of what awaits him on his return. Slowly, each of the family members in turn talks of Ollie and how special he was and how much fun they had with him and Elizabeth says, laughing bravely through her tears, that Ollie is playing even more now in his cat heaven than he did here on earth as he won't any longer have to stop for sleep. Peter had already called Thomas, their other older cat, over to inspect Ollie's body so that he wouldn't mourn, as a previous cat of theirs, Bethany, had mourned for her dead feline companion Toby. Thomas doesn't hang about though; he scuttles over the wall and into an adjacent field. Just before the committal of Ollie's body into the hole in the ground Peter says he must get something. Because I am worried he is going to wrap the cat in a shroud of some kind which will slow up the process of decomposition, I ask him warily 'what?' and he just replies quietly:

'A cross.' I am embarrassed by my brutish intervention for even asking. Ollie is buried with great dignity in the ground wearing a silver cross round his neck and with a catnip toy between his paws which he had played with in the ten happy months that he had spent as a member of this loving family. As the final turf is replaced over the mound under which he lies, Thomas suddenly reappears on the wall, and watches, sphinx-like, the final stamping down of the grave. No one present is really sure whether Thomas has or hasn't  'registered' that it was Ollie and that he was dead – time will tell. Thomas and Ollie were not always the best of friends but that doesn't mean that Thomas will be free of grief for his housemate. As we talk I bewail the frequency of road death for cats, but Hilary then tells me that of the five cats they have lived with over twenty-two years, Ollie is in fact the first to be killed by a car.

'We have a cat flap and they are free to come and go as they please, day or night. We believe that this village is a safe village.'

I discover from Michael afterwards that Ollie's body was found just by the bridge on Gallowber Lane,[40] the quietest single-track road out of the

---

[40] known as Gallowber as, at one time, sheep rustlers were hanged from the gallows at the lane end as an appalling example to their fellow men of their wrong-doing.

village, which is only a few hundred yards from where he was first discovered as a kitten on Halloween last year and that Peter bravely carried his stiff little body home cradled in a towel.

As Michael drives me back up the hill I hear once more in my inner ear the anguish in Hilary's voice as she whispered:

'I cannot believe I will never again receive that Ollie welcome that he gave us every morning.'

🐾 🐾 🐾

The very next day I have an appointment to take Gilly to see Gerard, the vet, as I have been concerned for some time that her chronic diarrhoea may be harmful to her, even though I am aware she has always had a sensitive stomach, and now she is having loose bowel movements *outside* the cat litter tray rather than in it, but a further cause for concern is that her back legs are noticeably lacking in hair and her front legs are nearly as bad and so is the area under her tail. As I bundle up my black (and now white in parts) moth-eaten 'fluff ball', who is still so innocent of trips to the vet and other hated car journeys that she is actually sitting on the cat-carrying basket, eager for an adventure, I feel a sharp, albeit pointless pang of guilt that my black Halloween cat is alive and Ollie down the road is not and as I pass over the bridge where he was run over I feel an overwhelming sense of sadness.

Gerard gives her an antihistamine injection but also takes a slide of her hairs to confirm under a microscope that it is 'self-abuse', i.e. she is tearing out her own fur, rather than it just spontaneously dropping out, and the following day he confirms to me that she is, but by this time I know that too as she is licking and licking repeatedly, something I should have realised myself earlier. On our return home I let her out into the garden and go off to attend to the hens. As I am refilling their bucket of water I hear from across the road a series of furious and oft-repeated wails, almost bellows, from Gilly from somewhere right in the middle of the garden. The noise she is making is extraordinary. She is really yelling and I can hear Michael talking back to her. I return to the garden and find Michael shaking with laughter.

'She is completely outrageous. That noise you heard was her shouting from plain bad temper.'

'Why? I was transfixed when I first heard it; they could have heard it up at Lupton!'

'I came out when I first heard her racket: she was standing looking down at a dead shrew and just yelling at it because it wouldn't move, and then she moved forward and flung it up in the air with her front foot and let it drop down and got even crosser when it remained where it fell. I'm afraid it has had a bin-burial!'

The next day I go back to the surgery as Gerard is enthusiastically committed to eliminating everything that can be wrong with Gilly. He is doubly concerned about her chronic diarrhoea and her 'self-abuse' which he still feels are unrelated, and this trip is for me to collect the antibiotic for her bowel. Because Gilly is a difficult patient we have agreed to administer the antibiotic in liquid form to be squeezed into her mouth via a small syringe without a needle.

When Michael and I attempt to administer the antibiotic it is nothing like as simple as we had imagined and in the end we have to resort to the time-honoured tradition of wrapping Gilly in a towel to stop her clawing us and between us squidging in the antibiotic. She hates it and spits it straight out again so I am covered in it all. The next day we try again, and very slowly we get the medicine down her. She makes a wonderful, love-able, gulping, half-drowning noise which disarm-ingly sounds like the noise she makes when she really loves some good food – a sort of loud combination of 'yum, yum, yum' followed by a gulping plea for help, which this time, when we put her on the floor, is followed with 'yow, yow, yow' and then followed by violent vomiting which in its turn is followed by more baleful complaints. After this she shuffles off to her bed with a tragic air and I follow her and watch her go into a deep sleep.

I come back downstairs and Michael nudges me: 'Look at this.' I turn round and there is Fannie trotting, yes trotting, up and down the conser-vatory with her nose in the air and full of confidence.

'I can't remember the last time I saw Fannie bouncing round like that inside the house,' I observe mournfully.

'That's true, but there couldn't have been a cat in the village, never mind the house, who didn't hear

Gilly's "dying swan" performance, and Fannie has come down to celebrate.'

'That's awful,' I giggle, but it is spot on. She comes up to me quietly making her special miaow and I pick her up in my arms and cuddle her, mumbling into the top of her head:

'Fannie, you don't have to be quite so shockingly buoyant.' She just purrs, deeply.

The next day Peter Warner comes to stay for a few days. His aim is to reacquaint himself with the cats and in Gilly's case to meet her for the first time; to do feline life drawings; to meet some of the people in the village whose own cat tales have become intermingled with the tales of the Coach House cats; to become more familiar with the surrounding lie of the land and to work out the new jacket.

Early on in his visit he watches Michael and me wrestling with Gilly in the feeding of her antibiotics and he quietly shows us a better way. He gently bends both her ears back under his hand which he holds there: this successfully distracts her and after squeezing half the dose of medicine into her mouth, he stops and strokes her throat to help her swallow and then continues. It works. She still gulps and makes her yum, yum, yum noises, but she has taken it all and hasn't spat it back and isn't sick. However, as soon as we release her she shuffles off, in case we decide to give her more, and yet again we are regaled by the sight of Fannie strutting the length of the conservatory in triumph at Gilly's indisposition.

I am beguiled by Peter's observation as an artist of the extraordinary shine of Gilly's coat. He says that the shine and the blackness is like ebony and it has the density of treacle, which is, I realise now, of course why Beth must have called her beloved black Bengal boy 'Treacle'. He is amused at her feistiness also, and of course, being the human-loving Bengal cat she is, she plays to the gallery. However, on his second day here I hear him murmuring to Pushkin:

'I think, Pushkin, you really are my favourite, you know.' Pushkin responds warmly by head-butting Peter's hand a couple of times.

'Peter, I am shocked at you, you're not supposed to have favourites.'

'Oh, I know, but he's so friendly. There really *has*

been a remarkable change in him since I last saw him.'

And I reflect that when Peter was last here Pushkin was still in the last stages of his trauma from the move and he hated being here, and now he loves it probably more than any of them and he is more and more adventurous and wandering further and further away all the time. We achieve much in Peter's visit and after he has gone I think that I sense the cats missing him around. He is almost certainly the only houseguest they have experienced who openly welcomes their lounging around on his bed so that he can sketch them from early morning until late at night.

One small incident that happens while Peter is here makes me catch my breath. While I am showing him some significant landmarks in the middle of the village and we are standing just outside Hutton Roof Hall, I suddenly turn round, having talked about the tragic death of Ollie, and there is a black cat sitting bang in the middle of the road in defiance of all traffic. As I stare at him the cat gets up, shakes a leg and walks off. It is, I discover, Samson who, together with his female companion Delilah, lives with Anthony and Jacky Chaplow and their two children, Josie and Scott.

Shortly after Peter drives away on his long trek back to the South-east, Gilly has a noisy 'woe-is-me' bout of diarrhoea around my newly planted rose (Rosa New Dawn, a lovely fragrant pale pearl-pink double climber, which I am longing to see spill up and over the wall) and, in a rather emphatic display of relief following it, she races out from under the rose and halfway across the garden, just for the hell of it, stops and instead gives Fannie a comprehensive chasing. Fannie runs into the house, ears flattened and hissing madly, and Gilly chases her upstairs, whereupon she flees into my study. Pushkin and Titus are both downstairs and have watched this performance in that peculiarly feline manner of being only mildly interested, but as Gilly chases upstairs, Pushkin becomes more animated and chases on up after her. I don't see what happens, but quite shortly afterwards Pushkin comes downstairs again and Gilly follows. Pushkin, realising he is being followed, lies down on his side on the bend in the stairs beating his tail animatedly and watches her, wanting to play. Gilly with consummate grace sidesteps him and moves into the kitchen to eat. After she has refuelled sufficiently she comes back and starts to walk upstairs past him. He bats her gently but playfully on the head with his right foreleg. Surprisingly she backs off, but then he starts to chase her and she runs upstairs, but she stays up there and won't join in his quite clear invitation to play.

The relationship between them changes all the time, as do the places where they rest. It depends on climate, ascendancy and mood; whether I am in front of my computer where three of them sleep usually and, most significantly of all, whether I have lit a fire in the sitting-room. We have the central heating on low in the evenings now and really do not need a fire as well, but it is such a cheerful thing to have and, if anyone is staying and it is remotely cool, I light a fire and then the status quo is radically altered. Gilly is the first to grab it, stretched flat out, full length on the rug slap in front of it like a small black dog. Fannie and Titus will then take the sofa opposite and Pushkin joins them on the arm of it. I love it when all four cats are in there like that. Then it is perfect. Not much room for people but great feline karma!

CHAPTER 19

The field immediately opposite our house, behind the hen paddock, is owned by Ian and Elizabeth, who live at the bottom of the hill. Shortly after we first moved in, Ian and Elizabeth came up to visit us, and as Ian was admiring the view from our window in due deference to our ecstasy at what we overlooked, I will never forget the following exchange:

'You do realise that that field out there is mine.'

'Yes, I do. But hey, Ian, why are you saying it in that funny way?'

'Well, it's really good we've seen you tonight because I wasn't sure when I would catch you to tell you that we're seriously thinking of growing a leylandii hedge along the back boundary of your little yard and our field as a wind break.'

I looked up at him in horror. His field is what we look straight over towards Ingleborough and the Yorkshire Dales. It was only when I saw the sparkle of laughter in his eyes, and his mouth twisted up in barely controlled mirth that I was fully reassured that he was winding us up. We were easy meat for him that night!

For some years Ian has leased this field to Harold[41] from the other end of the village, who in fact built the sturdy dry stone wall around the hen paddock as a commission for Pamela when it was a plant nursery. Harold kept sheep on it at various times of the year, but now he has semi-retired and moved away and so for most of this year Ian has been letting it out to Sue and Richard, who farm land all around us and who live right in the middle of the village. I have enjoyed watching the, to me, unusual

---

[41] who was at one time the official village cat grave digger and who also once told us that when he was younger he dreamed about getting enough money to buy the house we now live in 'but it just went and got too big' as subsequent owners added bits to it!

assortment of sheep and sometimes cattle that have been steadily grazing it. I am used to the old Dales way (pre-Foot-and-Mouth) of sheep-farming, which typically consisted of flocks of hardy Swaledale ewes with their black masks and white muzzles and curly horns, who every November were put to the larger, but much more tender roman-nosed Blue-faced Leicester tups. The lambs they fathered would be born from April onwards, to be sold at the auction marts if they were male as 'fat' lambs, or 'store' lambs from July on or, if they were gimmers (female), to farmers 'from down-country' for breeding in the exclusive Mule Sheep Association gimmer lamb sales in September. Although these lambs are called (confusingly) 'Mules', they are fertile and not at all mule-like in any way and are good breeders, good mothers and make good meat. Now, however, as I look out at Ian's field opposite I see it is full of Texel tups, a breed completely new to me, with deliciously funny faces. Their heads are completely white, but they have black nose leather and black lips and they always peer at you slightly myopically along their noses, which somehow gives them the appearance of grinning – this is enhanced by their stiff ears which hang forwards at slightly skewed angles, giving them a rather disconnected look somehow. It is lovely to be surrounded by smiling sheep, even if it is only an illusion! As I watch them for several days I become galvanised and decide I must find out more about sheep farming this side of the hill as it is clearly a whole different ball game from how it was east of the Pennines. I phone the Pricketts up and rather cheekily persuade Sue to allow me to go farming with them one day and thus begins my instruction in animal husbandry in the Southern Lakes as, in common with most other farmers around here, they farm livestock exclusively, although Sue does have another string to her bow, which interests me greatly.

I drive down to the Prickett farmstead in the middle of the village, recognisable from a distance by its oval hanging sign rather like a pub sign, which on one side shows a Texel tup in bas relief surrounded by the inscription Hutton Roof Hall and on the other side the name again but this time encompassing a Limousin bull. Over the front door of the beautiful stone-built house is a Victorian date stone above the lintel stating 1869. I walk round to the side door and am greeted by a bonny, slim, smiling young woman who, with her glowing cheeks, is the very embodiment of health and who is the mistress of all that I survey. Sue, who has pulled the short straw labelled 'teacher' as Richard is busy baling, takes my lesson in hand immediately and I learn from her, and then more later from my Dales friend, Thomas, that everything has indeed changed on both sides of the hill since the country was swept by the scourge of Foot and Mouth Disease in 2001. The new trend in sheep farming, even in comparatively high pastures like the Cumbrian fells, is to concentrate on producing stock that can go straight to the market for meat rather than risk the process of breeding and passing on to other farmers in milder climes to fatten up the stock. During the Foot and Mouth epidemic many sheep farmers, those who managed to stay in it, were forced by the restriction of movement of stock to breed from their own Mules, rather than stick with the traditional Swaledales or Rough Fells, and this led to a diversification of stockholding, which is why I am now all at sea when I view the sheep around me. Sue takes me round some of the many acres that she and Richard farm and shows me with pride their Texel tups, which are terminal sires bred for their exceptional carcass qualities. I discover too that the Texel ewe is hardy and exceptionally thrifty and her lambs have a tremendous get-up-and-go attitude, seeking milk as soon as they are born.

Richard and Sue will also put their Texels tups to Lleyn, Rough Fell and Texel ewes and their Rough Fell tups to Rough Fell and Blackface ewes. As I am digesting this information Sue points out a Texel gimmer which they have decided they will put with their 'Klintup' as they have just one of these amongst their gang of Texel and Rough Fell boys.

'What on earth is a Klintup?' I ask.

'A Lleyn tup? Well, it's a breed which originated in North Wales. L-L-E-Y-N!' Sue spells out for me patiently. 'We use that Lleyn tup to produce the Lleyn/Texel crosses I was talking about.'

I had seen the name on paper but never heard it pronounced. This learning business is difficult for both parties! But Sue is wonderful and is not off-put by my daft questions and continues her tuition with a litany of other sheep crosses that they produce. Originally they had produced Mashams before they started to breed their own Texel tups – in fact her father had crossed a Charollais tup with a Texel Ewe to use the tup lamb with his Welsh Mule ewes – but now with their own flock of Texel tups they cross Texels with Rough Fells, Hill Cheviots, North Country Cheviots, Texels and all crosses in between. They did cross a Border Leicester tup with a Texel ewe for several years to try to get a sheep that produced more lambs – although Border Leicesters don't live as long as the hardy Texels. At the end of this long list of crosses I ask Sue about Herdwicks and she says, predictably:

'Ah, yes, we also have a few Herdwicks crossed with Texels.' It is the Herdwicks in particular that I want to know about as they are unique to the Lakes – with their white faces and browny/grey exceptionally waterproof fleeces – having a legendary instinct for 'hefting'[42] – although there are a few around here in other farmers' flocks. Every year out of the lambs that are born Richard and Sue will keep around 120 gimmers as replacements for their current stock and they will aim to keep those gimmers that were born as one of two or more so that the multiple birth 'gene' might be passed on. They have used Blackface tups too but have given them up since they suffered cruelly from Toxoplasmosis passed on, supposedly, from foxes on the crag, or possibly feral cats. I know that it is a parasite that afflicts cats but hadn't realised it could be passed to other mammals and have since discovered that *Toxoplasma gondii* can infect all warm-blooded animals but an essential stage of its life-cycle occurs only in cats. In sheep it causes abortions.

---

[42] a northern hill-farming term for sheep who stick to the same hillside, who know precisely what bit is their home patch without aid of fences. Herdwicks are particularly likely to become hefted into an area and the cull during the Foot and Mouth epidemic is said to have destroyed 40 per cent of the national flock of Herdwicks.

During this tour we have travelled from pasture to pasture in Richard and Sue's Jeep. We now drive down the single-track Gallowber Lane, over the  little bridge where poor little Ollie was killed and turn right through a field gate and bumpily make our way up into a high pasture, which climbs ever higher up through woodland and beyond until we find ourselves on top of a grassy hill in the middle of nowhere. The views from there make my eyes fill up for the pure pleasure of being alive and being able to stand and stare at this rural paradise. As we climb out of the Jeep on the summit we hear above us a skylark[43] singing his heart out in wonderful liquid trilling chirrups and my soul soars the skies with him. The perspective of all our neighbours and their land and their houses is completely different from this angle and I spend a happy half-hour while Sue patiently points out who is what and where.

---

[43] Alauda arvensis

As well as all the sheep, Richard and Sue also keep a suckler herd, which essentially means that they are involved in beef farming, rather than dairy farming, which these days is increasingly thankless. Their stock consists of Limousin bulls, some pure bred cows and some crosses, including Angus and Angus-x-Friesians, Belgian Blue-x-Friesians and Salers, originally from the mountains of the Auvergne – and like some of the continental sheep this last is a new breed to me, but they are well suited to the rain-swept hillsides of the Westmorland Fells.

We finally return to the large welcoming farmhouse kitchen where I meet one of their five cats. This one is called Wunky and she is a four-year-old neutered female, mainly white with patches of tortie colouring, who has a disarming wheeze that Sue thinks might be the legacy of some flu she contracted when a very small kitten. It never gets worse and it never goes away. She and her neutered sister Tigger, a white-bibbed tabby, are the two cats that sleep in the farmhouse. The other three, called in ascending order of age Tabby Tom (two years old), Big Tom Cat (five years old) and

The Fast Cat (very, very old and very, very unfriendly), are completely outside working cats and are nowhere to be seen because they are no doubt busy. Their two Border collies, Bev and Misty, are also absent, but almost certainly they are with their master. Just as we are sitting down, in wanders the missing Tigger who takes one look at me, decides I am no threat, and curls up on a cat bed in the corner. Tigger looks the picture of innocence but Sue wrinkles her nose.

'I've had to stop feeding the birds. Tigger, in particular, is just a devil with them. She's the only cat we've ever had who regularly catches swallows.'

'Blimey, fully grown ones?'

'Fully grown, out of the nest, young, old, you name it. She gets fat in the winter, but in the summer she is lithe and thin, from chasing after swallows. And when she goes out into the yard, they swoop down on her, and you can always tell from the alarm calls they make that Tigger is around and it is only Tigger, none of the other cats!' I look across at the gently sleeping feline with not inconsiderable respect. Cats are hunters and some are very good at it.

I now manage to get Sue to explain more about the other 'string' to her bow of being an ace farmer and midwife to cattle and sheep. The string in question started when she joined the WI and began to make marmalade and jellies. I presume she started this because she had such long lonely hours to fill or more likely because one of the truths in life is if you want a job done, ask a busy person! She went on from there to make more and more different jellies, chutneys, jams and other preserves, always whenever possible from locally grown produce and always seasonally, and started slowly to sell them through a local farm shop called Kitridding[44] in Lupton and then at Lucy's bistro in more distant Ambleside and Country Delights in Settle. In September 2004 she was awarded the highly prestigious and much-coveted award of North West Producer of the Year by the North West Fine Foods sponsored by Defra and Booths and she also won a Silver Award in the Great Tastes Award in the same summer. From an article in *Cumbria Life Magazine* she gained the title of 'The

---

[44] http://www.kitridding.co.uk/New/

Blackcurrant Queen' which has rather charmingly stuck. I have eaten some of her Tomato Chutney and her Seville Marmalade and they are indeed absolutely scrumptious. Often in the summer evenings I have seen her and Richard walking together with their two sheepdogs, laughing and talking, and from time to time Sue will stop and pick a plant from the hedgerow, which is presumably some useful ingredient to be added to one of her delicious home-made preserves. I do wish Richard and Sue and their sons Jim and Peter all the luck in the world with their enterprises.

CHAPTER 20

Michael and I are hoping that the signs we see of Fannie gaining in confidence are not just our own wishful thinking, but even though we both feel we recognise this, she clearly continues to have a distinct fearfulness of Gilly which never seems to leave her. Today as I am sitting in the downstairs cloakroom Fannie squeezes round the door companionably and jumps up on to the boiler and from there to the drier, which is atop the washing machine, and as I look up to the little mirror above the washbasin I see her eyes staring down into mine with a dark intense softness. I murmur: 'O Fannie, darling girl. I love you so much . . . so much.' My

 voice is low and meant only for her, but by that utterance and the manner of its delivery, I make my mistake. As I look back into her eyes in the mirror her head suddenly goes down, her body stiffens and her ears come forward at the most acute angle possible with an awesome concentration, and I know with complete certainty that, although out of my sight, Gilly has emerged and is coming round the door somewhere. Gilly, having heard my dulcet tones, has decided to see what gives. Within seconds we are both assailed by the fierce hissing that is Fannie's immediate reaction to Gilly on all occasions and, with a thump and a cry which morphs into a half-groan, Fannie leaps down and races out, chased closely by Gilly. Up they thunder, into my study overhead and I hear Fannie scramble up the filing cabinet, alternately hissing and squawking, and I know that she will have clambered into her little box. Gilly then promptly trots downstairs again and comes back

into the lavatory, tail waving victoriously. She looks up at me and blinks twice, owlishly, and then miaows demandingly in her deep strident voice. In deference to her wishes I turn on the cold tap in the basin and up she jumps to drink the running water she so enjoys. She shows no sign of remorse for her bad behaviour towards Fannie, although I have seen cats – in particular Fannie – feel such an emotion, but then from her point of view she, Gilly, was only playing a game, wasn't she?

It is late September and with a stab of remorse I realise that all the swallows have gone and that yet again I have failed to see the great migration of those intrepid travellers, although if I look around hard enough I will probably still find the tail-end charlies, the second brood, hanging on till they have fattened up enough for the long haul. Truth to tell, I miss it almost every year; only one year did I actually observe the day they flew – early that morning they were all there chittering away on the telegraph wires and by the afternoon I realised that they had gone, but even so, I still missed the precise moment of take-off. At the beginning of September I remember Sue Prickett shivering as she looked up and saw them gathering on the telegraph lines four deep like so many crotchets and quavers (only with the fifth stave missing).

'Why are you shuddering?' I asked, although the sight of them assembling in greater numbers, day by day, always saddens me too.

'Oh the earlier they go, the tougher our winter is going to be, they always say,' she laughed, but I understand full well her melancholy. In spite of our climate change and the long hot and intermittently damp summer, it is indeed early for our swallows to have gone, so we shall see what sort of a winter is to hit us.[45]

I have recently introduced another bird-feeding station into the garden with all manner of seeds, nuts and fat balls, although top choice is sunflower hearts, and am amused to see an extraordinary mixture of birds sitting on the splayed-out upward pointing boughs of the yew tree, like so many Christmas tree decorations clamped to the branches, blowing up and down in the wind. They are almost certainly checking to make sure there

---

[45] For information, it *was* a long cold winter.

are no cats around. As I look now from my window I can see four chaffinches, three green-finches, two thrushes, two blackbirds and a constantly changing number of great tits, blue tits and coal tits, and on the telephone line immediately outside the window are four goldfinches, who especially love sunflower hearts. The thrushes and the blackbirds, although they do visit the flat seed tray, are really in the yew because they are defending the ripe red berries which they are in the process of systematically devouring as they become soft enough. Yesterday I was thrilled to see two nuthatches on the nuts: their visits are spasmodic and I had thought seasonal, but I discover they are in fact actually resident here, year-round, but nesting up in the woodland. They are timid, and certainly visit less frequently than their equally bashful larger cousins, the great spotted woodpecker, two of which regularly 'hit' the nuts, for a few brightly coloured seconds.

This should have been a good year for insect-ivorous birds as the insect life has been abundant – not only has there been a surfeit of the now detested harvest mites but also scourges of mosquitoes, midges, gnats, moths, blue-bottles, horseflies (aka clegs) and, of course, the common housefly have all been ever-present. Although not fodder for most garden birds, bumblebees this year have abounded and indeed they continue to bumble around even today, although our ears are no longer filled with the comforting sound of their heavy hums: you have to lean closely to them now to catch even one note of their diminuendo-hymn to autumn. That quiet hymn could be thought of as a requiem as the queen bumblebee, having produced unceasing numbers of workers since February or March, will recently have produced new queens and male non-workers who will by now have mated and, that having been done, all the males will die, as will the old queen, and the new queens will shortly go away to hibernate in order to produce next year's 'bike' of hardworking bumblebees. Although with bumblebees, as with so many other species, there is new evidence to suggest some colonies now are able to work over winter due to the warmer climate. On Monday, which turned into a glorious warm sunny day, Michael and I were enchanted to witness two sleepy bumblebees being joined on their nectar-hunt by no fewer than four red admiral butterflies[46] on the long white bottle-brush spikes of the fragrant autumn-flowering white pearl bugbane[47] so perhaps this kaleidoscopic quartet is going to risk hibernating here in Cumbria rather than migrating to Europe or North Africa. Hibernation for red admirals is common in the south of England, but I am unsure this far north. Their caterpillars love nettles and there are certainly plenty of those in the nearby hedgerows, although the adults now are nectar hungry and are supping copiously from not only the white pearl, which seems to be their preferred host of the moment, but also from the late-blooming dark violet buddleia[48] over by the gate, added to which they have the blackberries that are knitted into the hedge around two

---

[46] Vanessa atalanta
[47] Cimicifuga simplex
[48] Buddleia davidii

sides of the hens' paddock across the road from which to feast and, when all these are gone, they will be able to move on to the flowering ivy[49] that blankets our garden wall. I am constantly in awe at the considerable nursery skills of the former owner and creator of this garden, Pamela, who has relinquished to us a garden that is not only wildlife friendly and extremely attractive, but which also flowers almost year-round.

Thomas, who did such a fine job of rendering the chick coops into housing for laying hens, very generously offers to come and help Michael with the fencing around the paddock, so that I can at last let the hens out into a bigger space. The day that Thomas chooses is frustratingly for me one when I will be out doing signings at bookshops all day, but both he and Michael claim that they are glad that I won't be able to interfere with their day's labouring, which they call 'man's work', and I am also told that when I do come back I must on no account come in and behave like the foreman. What a hard brief! I organise a cold lunch for them both and, just before

---

[49] Hedera helix

I leave, Thomas pulls up in his Land Rover laden down with sixteen large round 6-foot-6-inch-long stakes, two sledge-hammers, nails, screws and other accoutrements for the job in hand. As he starts to unload he is laughing: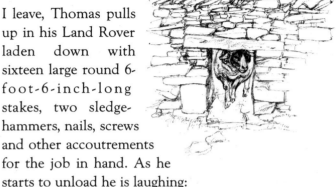

'Nay, I saw some sheep yonder using a thur'ole. It's a gey lang time since I saw one of them!'

'What's a "thurrell", Thomas?'

'Why a "thur'ole" or "thirl hole"[50] is a hole in a wall low down for sheep to pass *through* from one field into another, when mebbe the farmer doesn't want larger stock going through. You can block them up with a paving slab if you don't want the sheep passing through.'

As I take my leave of them they are already stuck into their day's work and when I return in mid-

---

[50] also called hogg hole, thawl, smout hole, sheep creep and sometimes cripple hole.

afternoon, they have just finished. There is a curiously conspiratorial air about them both, but the fruits of their labour look superb. I thank Thomas effusively for his toil and he replies:

'It was a great pleasure working with Michael, and we did a good job together.'

After he has gone Michael says in a wistful sort of voice:

'Today was a good day, you know. It was really nice working with Thomas, he's very good company. And blimey he's one strong man.'

When I get into the house there are two or three empty beer bottles on the side and the food has disappeared, so I presume that Michael looked after Thomas properly. With great ceremony we remove the dividing fence between the hens' coop, the tunnel and the extended paddock and the hens are now free to roam. They spend most of their time flying up on to the internal wall and back down again, but although they could fly up and over the fencing that Thomas and Michael so laboriously erected they don't, and seem content enough to settle down in their larger quarters.

Today is sparkling and bright and the sun is

already warm. I rush out as soon as I am awake to open up their ark and, sliding the door up and to one side, I talk the while to reassure them in response to their cackling and clucking protests coming from within. There then follows the usual unseemly scramble through the pop hole and down the ramp to get out, accompanied by the flexing of wings and running circuits round the ark to check all is as it was before they went to bed. This morning a couple of them captivate me by adopting, with great seriousness, the fighting posture of mature cockerels facing each other square on, each standing fully upright with neck stretched up to its tallest limit and at the same time pressing their puffed-out chests to each other, and touching the end of their beaks, so it is really quite hard for them to peer at each other from that angle. They hold this position for about thirty seconds before breaking away and scratching about as if nothing has happened. Sometimes as they pass each other I have noticed that if they feel threatened, they will fluff out their neck feathers at the base, which I recognise from Victorian paintings of fighting cocks and which is also reminiscent of hostile cats with their bottle-brush tails. I have had to buy corrugated plastic to cover the roof of the coop as in the torrential downpours we have intermittently been having, in spite of my earlier creosoting, rain has been leaking in. Today continues to be mild and sunny and I carefully inspect the 'green manure' for any signs of growth. I had planted out Hungarian rye,[51] Alsike clover,[52] sprouting clover organic, field beans,[53] giant winter spinach and winter cress. The turf which we laid three weeks ago is beginning to put down long white roots through into the soil so soon it should be well anchored, and my wild flower meadow is growing reasonably well, although the fescue grasses do look very delicate so I fear how they will stand up to the hens' foraging.

🐾 🐾 🐾

Today I receive a sad email which has an extraordinary follow up to it.

---

[51] Secale Cereale
[52] Trifolium Hybridum
[53] Vicia Faba

From: Amanda Jane
To: Marilyn Edwards
Sent: Monday, October 03, 10:28 PM
Subject: Re: New reader

Dear Marilyn,

Your book certainly got to me, yes, because I lost my cat called Dali a year ago . . . Dali was 3–4 years old when I got him from the Cat Protection League (he was mainly black with white socks and neck). He lived with me, as an indoor cat, for 6 years in total. He was never a sickly cat, slept with me every night (head on pillow and covered with the quilt or curled up in the arch of my back) and that is where he would stay until morning.

He was an unassuming cat but very affectionate and especially good at knowing when I needed a cuddle.

The last couple of years of his life he was prone to getting small, benign cysts just above his eyes (I think 4 in total); he would have quick, routine operations and have them removed without any problem.

In October last year I took him to have another

lump/cyst removed. I took him to the vet's on the Monday night so he was there to have the operation first thing on the Tuesday morning. It was a new vet who I had the consultation with and who would be carrying out the operation – I took an instant dislike to him as he seemed over-confident and even a bit 'cocky'.

As I signed the consent form for the operation I had a sick feeling in my stomach. I then said goodbye to my gorgeous Dali and returned to my car where I sat and cried, having second thoughts about leaving him there.

I didn't feel any better on the morning of the operation but was patient and telephoned the surgery at 12.00 p.m. as suggested by the vet. I was told that Dali was still 'under' and to ring again at 1.00 p.m. The next hour seemed to last a lifetime. When I telephoned I was told by the veterinary nurse that Dali had come to nicely and that I could collect him in an hour (I was so relieved he was okay and excited about collecting him).

I reached the surgery and rang the bell (thinking it slightly odd that nobody was on reception). I was then met by the vet who was trying to tell me that Dali had collapsed 2 mins before I had arrived (after coming to completely from the anaesthetic). He was almost hysterical, making very odd laughing noises. In shock, I understood him to be making Dali better and that he had everything under control – I was clearly not hearing what he was really saying – Dali had already died!

You will not believe it, but a year has gone by and I still haven't been able to collect Dali's ashes – cannot bring myself to do it (if indeed they are still there) . . . they carried out a postmortem as they have to in such a situation but they found no reason why he died when he did . . . I was simply told that it's something that can just happen, although extremely rare. I also cannot find it in myself to forgive the vet . . . So, that's the story behind the tears . . .

Best wishes,
Amanda

Amanda, in her email, goes on to say that she has and loves dearly two British shorthair females called Hegel (someone else with a sexing problem!) and Ruby, but that does not, of course, heal the wounds of no longer having her beloved Dali.

A few weeks later I email Amanda, urging her to try to collect the ashes and asking her permission for me to use her email in the book. Twenty-four hours after sending the email I receive this amazing sequel:

— — —

From: Amanda Jane
To: Marilyn Edwards
Sent: Wednesday, November 09, 7:52 PM
Subject: Re: An extract?

Hi again Marilyn,
Just had to tell you that following our communications yesterday, my partner Paul rang me at work today to let me know that he had received a telephone call from the vet's, about Dali's ashes!!!! After a whole year! They were apparently very nice on the phone and just wanted to get a message to me to let me know that they still had the ashes and that I could go in and collect them if I wanted to!

I find the whole thing very strange, especially after your email (and as I said I was sure they had probably got rid of them). So after work I collected Dali and he is back home, albeit in a less than impressive box! Although I wouldn't share this with just anyone, I am convinced that it was a message from him . . . almost that he approves of his story being included in your book. It's just all so bizarre, but wonderful at the same time.

Just thought you would like to know . . .

Amanda

CHAPTER 21

It is early October, I am on my own and I am being unremittingly assailed by Gilly. She is on heat. She has been calling loudly for the last two days and, more to the point, for the last two nights and Michael, lucky chap, has missed it all by dint of being in Scotland with Johnny and Oliver. This is the first time that Gilly has come into season, and on the first night I was rather bemused as I thought she was yowling for Michael, as she divides her favours between us equally and will lie as often stretched out next to him as to me. It did disconcert me that so brief an absence was causing her this amount of distress. But as I lay in the dark

275

being plagued by her wails, the sounds changed key and became more guttural in their pitch and more urgent in their delivery. Total recall of how it was with Fannie's last heat overwhelms me, and I realise that this is no feline anxiety for a missing human companion: this is far more primeval and driven. Gilly's 'normal' voice is a rasping one, but her 'calling' voice has to be heard to be believed and sleep is quite impossible when she is in full cry.

When I told Michael about it on the phone on Sunday morning I think it is what tipped him into staying on an extra night with his boys. Anyway now I am stuck with it. I email the breeders and ask them if they still have their stud available and whether I can bring her up to them. They phone me back to say that although normally they would prefer that it be a second heat for a first mating, as she is nearly a year old and therefore presumably close to fully grown and developed, this heat should be OK and that, yes, their stud is available. Although they are aware that I know that Gilly has not been mated they still require that I take her down to the vet's and get her fully tested for FeLV and FIV. I explain about her allergy to harvest mite, but they don't see that as an impediment, and since her course of antibiotic when Peter Warner was here (and also since restricting her diet to either Hills Dried Adult Cat or Burns Dried Adult only) her bowels have sorted themselves out, so that is no longer a problem. I make an appointment at the vet's and discuss her health with Paul when I take her down, and he agrees with the breeders that everything is fine and the breeding can go ahead. He shaves a great big square patch of fur from her throat to do the blood tests, which gives moth-eaten little Gilly an even stranger look still, and after a suitable waiting time he reports back that the results of the test are negative.

Michael returns home from Scotland and we discuss all that is happening at length. We are both really excited at the prospect of Gilly's impending family. I am due to take Gilly to the breeders in forty-eight hours' time. I phone Peter Warner and tell him that this is all taking place, just to check that he still wants a kitten from her. He enthusiastically confirms that he does. It has always been agreed between us that if there is a choice of gender, Peter should have a female kitten who would be more likely to get on better with Blue, his neutered tom. As we are talking Peter then adds that, in time, he would quite like to breed from the kitten himself. I repeat to him that the deal I have with the breeders is that the offspring of Gilly may not be bred from, but he still says he would like the possibility of considering it, and so I tell him I will talk to the breeders. I duly phone the breeders and because I mention the active list they are immediately very unhappy that I am even asking them. I quickly say I understand and that I will go back to Peter and explain that it is not going to be possible, which I do, and Peter takes it on board and agrees completely with all that they ask, although he is of course disappointed. I go back assuring the breeders that all will be well and so it is with extreme dismay that evening that I find an email from them, the main message of which is:

'We are very sorry but we have decided that we

cannot go ahead with the mating.' Michael and I are devastated. Michael in fact becomes quite angry. I just feel desperate and let down, but, stirred up by Michael's anger, I email back, really upset, saying I feel betrayed. I receive a reply saying that they will pay for Gilly's FeLV test if that will help, but that for the moment their answer is still that they would rather not do the mating, but that they are prepared to consider some time in the future 'some arrangement that is amicable all ways round. What that may be at present, we just don't know'. It is all so vague and it doesn't resolve the problem of the here and now, and so I feel I need to take time out to think about it all. When I was first looking for Gilly there was another breeder further south who was really helpful and he said to me then that if I ever needed a Bengal stud I should consider approaching him. Michael and I talk long and hard about whether we should do that.

Gilly is still rampaging around and calling fit to wake the dead and for two nights I sleep very little. On my second sleepless night I find myself praying intensely for guidance and for peace and suddenly at around 4.30 a.m. I fall asleep, very deeply. When the light wakes me in the morning inside my head I know the answer. At breakfast I say to Michael that I've been thinking. He groans. He always groans when I say that, it's strange!

'How many cats do we have at the moment?'

'You know jolly well we have four, why are you asking daft questions like this?'

'Oh, because this is an exercise, go on indulge me.'

'Huh, when don't I? Alright, next?'

'If Gilly has kittens, how many do you think we would keep here?'

'That's like how long is a piece of string: it depends on how many she has, but I imagine you would want to keep at least two knowing you.'

'Which would mean how many cats would we have here then?'

'Six, by my reckoning.'

'And three of them would be Bengals. How do you think Fannie would react to that?'

'She would probably have a nervous breakdown, pack her bags and leave home, or top herself, but what is daft about your questions now, is that you knew all this all along.'

'No, what is different now, is that I've seen, we have both seen, how really bad it is for Fannie with Gilly, in a way it never was when Pushkin came, for example.'

'Yes, that's true,' he says thoughtfully.

'I just feel, Michael, sometimes things happen, or don't happen for a reason. I couldn't understand why that couple, who are basically good people, have gone back on their word in this way, even when I assured them that Peter would adhere to everything they asked, but now I feel it's as if it is for a reason. If we had been going to have kittens from Gilly, it had to be this year for the kitten to be any companion to Blue for Peter, and the same was true for Janice – she wanted the kitten sooner rather than later – and for us too. We've been trying to have kittens for over three years now. And it feels to me, right now, as if this is God directly saying, "Don't do it."'

Michael goes quiet for a little while and then very gently he agrees. It is strange but for him too, as for me, it is as if there is writing on the wall. I email the breeders and tell them that I will get Gilly spayed and I phone the vet as soon as they are open.

Gerard is on holiday so we have to wait a little while, but I book her in.

Gilly calls for nearly two weeks and her voice becomes daily hoarser from her abuse of it, so that she now sounds like a feline equivalent of Edith Piaf emitting that wonderful guttural cracked rendering of 'Non, je ne regrette rien', only in Gilly's case it is exceedingly difficult to determine what she may or may not regret. And she is so different when she is on heat – not least because she stops threatening Fannie. To begin with Fannie doesn't trust this change and continues to hiss whenever she sees Gilly, but finally they are able to be in the same room, on the same sofa, without friction. The truth is Gilly is barely remembering to eat.

I remember how desperate it was for Titus and for Fannie when they both came on heat, and in the last stages for Fannie it was almost unbearable, which triggered my searching out her stud boy and then finally resorting to having her neutered. Now, here, for Gilly it is again so hard for her. I can hardly bear seeing her distress. As I pick her up in my arms and try to cradle her, instead of her lying flexibly on her back staring up at me, as she would normally, she stretches out her body full length, in a strange, rigid pose and her eyes have a distant look while she makes a rasping moaning cry. She is so altered from how she is normally. The date for her hysterectomy is in the diary two weeks from today.

I am in my study working away at my desk and have let the three older cats out into the garden but have carefully shut the door so that Gilly cannot join them, as while I am sure there are no full toms around it would be foolhardy to risk her becoming pregnant at this stage. Suddenly, through my study window I can hear Gilly's cries, rasping and raucous and very

angry-sounding coming apparently from outside. I rush downstairs and I can still hear her carrying on and then it goes quiet. I run up the other flight of stairs into our bedroom and see her walking across the bed, scratching repeatedly at the duvet. The window with the cat guard is wide open and that is why it had sounded as if she was outside: she must have seen the other cats in the garden and was expressing her frustration with some force. I look at the duvet cover and realise, suddenly, that it is soaking wet. In her disturbed state she has urinated, with an apparently full bladder, right through the duvet, through the sheet, the undersheet, the mattress cover and the mattress. I strip the bedding down as fast I can, wash the mattress and cover the bed with a series of long strips of bubble-wrap. We have an enormous bed so washing the enormous duvet requires an industrial washing machine, for which we have to go down to the town . The following day we are out very late and on our return crash into bed and sleep heavily. In the morning we sleep late, but suddenly Michael shouts out:

'I don't believe it, she's at it again, right now!'

And sure enough she has just left another huge puddle right where Michael was sleeping. Again we strip the bed down and this time I am able to wash the smaller temporary duvet at home. I remember how much anxiety Hilary had when her little Ollie did this a couple of times on their bed, and it is, indeed, very disturbing. Our added problem is that there is no door to our bedroom and no way of blocking out any cat who wants to come in. Needless to say, on the third morning she attempts to do the same thing again and we just manage to stop her. Her ardour seems to have lessened a little, as she is only waking us twice during the night now, whereas before she was calling every hour or so. Michael asks me:

'Will the neutering definitely stop this impossible behaviour?'

'Oh Michael, I just pray it will. I'm sure it's because she's so frustrated, but the only trouble is the hormonal change takes a while before it kicks in and she has been spraying outside. She's the first female cat I have seen who sprays like a tom, although I always knew they can do it.'

The following day I wake up early and am

nervous that she may repeat the performance and to crack 'the syndrome' seems to me paramount, so I take the risk of impregnation and let her out. I open the door wide and the air smells wonderful. It is a glorious mild sunny day and the hills look magnificent in their purple and gold livery. All four cats go bounding out joyously. After about an hour Pushkin, Titus and Fannie return and lounge around the conservatory happily, idly watching the birds at the feeders, but 'Black Magic' remains out for a good four hours. Michael goes to help Richard with his mammoth task of leaf clearance next door, when he learns that at some point in her travels she has been sighted by Richard round the back of his garden, which we are all trying to teach her is strictly forbidden. 'Forbidden', however, is a concept which seems quite alien to young Gilly.

Gilly wakes up the following day, at exactly 7.15 a.m., having lain next to me all night without stirring. I hear her go downstairs and I assume she is using the cat litter tray. Lying in a state of semi-sleep, I become aware of her quiet return as she springs lightly onto the bed and I open one eye to see her surveying Michael's sleeping form and

then, before I can stop her, she forcefully empties a full bladder all over him, the duvet et al. Things are uttered by us both which no human should ever say to a companion cat, much loved or otherwise, and the washing machine and the dryer are brought back into full eco-unfriendly operation yet again.

Then, the next day, although she is still doing her feline imitation of Piaf in a half-hearted way when she remembers to, she visibly goes 'off the boil'. Fannie trots past her in her new reassured confident manner, and Gilly slowly hunches her shoulders, puts her head down and does 'the stare'. Fannie is transparently horrified – and in a different way so am I. Before I know what is happening Gilly has chased Fannie upstairs, and all is as it was before. Indeed, it is worse than before. Later in the day, while sitting at my computer, I hear an unfamiliar scratching noise. I turn round to look. To my horror I see Gilly just disappearing into Fannie's special box on top of the filing cabinet. Fannie, while this is happening, is downstairs eating.

'No, Gilly! That's the Holy of Holies. You cannot go in there.' I climb up the library steps, reach in and pull her out and plonk her on the floor. Immediately she starts her ascent again. She does it by climbing up the bookshelves rather than springing up from the top of the steps as Fannie does it, so at least for now, by moving books around, I can make it impossible for her to repeat this.

Gilly, post-heat, now seems to be asserting territorial rights. She singles out whichever chair is Titus's favourite and lies on it, in front of Titus. If Titus isn't in the room, then she doesn't bother. Pushkin still tries to sneak round the back of the stairs in Michael's study where he hid when we first moved here, and the other day I found Gilly lurking in there too.

One thing that Gilly does that is quite beguiling is to lie on top of the cat platform in the conservatory staring out of the window, but when you go up to her, she gives you what I call her veiled look. Although on other occasions she does give you direct eye contact – she even does the dreadful stare, which is seriously threatening – when she is in her modest mode she seems to go to some lengths to avoid holding direct eye contact, so as you approach her on her platform she holds her head down in the coy manner of a woman from a culture where she has been taught never to make eye contact – Gilly the bashful. Gilly the modest. Gilly the games player.

CHAPTER 22

It is now the end of October and over the last few weeks the rain has been intermittent, but when it has come, it has been torrential and the polythene tunnel has come into its own as the hens' shelter. I have recently introduced a deep litter of wood shavings into the tunnel, which they adore and they spend more time in there, dust bathing in the shavings and in the compost, than they do on the open grass in the paddock proper. I had imagined that once I let them out into the main paddock they would never come in, but the tunnel is definitely their favourite place even on dry days. They feel safe in there too, I think. As well as hating the rain,

they are not keen on having their feathers ruffled up too much either, and although it is still astonishingly mild the autumn winds are gusting almost every day now, bringing down the leaves from the many trees that surround the house. The gutters keep filling up and overflowing with leaves so that the rain spills over the edges and pours down the windows of the conservatory like a solid waterfall. Michael has already been round the whole of the outside of the house with his step-ladder clearing them out, but there are still many more leaves to fall, and fall they do. As we look out through the windows they come spiralling down, some seemingly so desirous of making their land-fall that they jostle and somersault past others which are on a more leisurely trajectory. This unre-lenting 'confetti', which has been happening for days, just reinforces to me the truly staggering number of leaves each tree produces. The leaf-fall is deeply attractive to worms, who take cover beneath the mounting piles, and today as I walk out with the hens' food in my hand, having kicked a pile of leaves to one side, I spot a particularly large and juicy looking specimen and put him on the hens' warm mash to give to them as a treat. When I get across the road and into the tunnel where I feed the hens, I am belatedly overcome with remorse at the fate I am delivering to this harmless creature, so I hastily toss him away into the now quite long grass in the paddock, in the hope that this will enhance his odds of surviving. The hens fail to notice their 'treat' flying through the air, so at least for this day he does indeed get away.

Although I have kept hens in the past I am astonished anew at the bullying that goes on between them and it is so unfair too, as the biggest and the strongest gang up on the smallest and youngest, with no one hen prepared to defend her coop mate in distress. It is said that cockerels keep their girls in check and prevent this bad behaviour, but I have never owned one so I cannot vouch for it. The youngest and most got-at hen I call Emily and her tail is tattered and scruffy, which I was putting down to the moult they have all been going through, but I have just recently noticed that two of the others pull her tail feathers out each time they are close to her. Rather like Fannie with Gilly she is her own worst enemy, however, as whenever she comes near the others she goes on autopilot and starts to squawk and rush around attracting enormous attention to herself, so even the hens who would have ignored her are almost compelled to give her a passing tweak or stab. They adore raisins and all of them come over to eat out of my hand. They also do that hen curtsey, which they properly do for the cockerel, so he might mount them, but which in the absence of a cockerel they do for the alpha being. It is useful that they do it, as it means it is easier to pick them up and give them an examination or, more likely, a cuddle from time to time.

It feels terrible that Avian flu might be creeping closer and I get so depressed by the prevailing view that it is simply a matter of when rather than if. Tonight I was standing in the tunnel just putting the feed away for the night and outside a blackbird was singing that long lyrical dusk song of eventide and the thought that all this rich bird life could be under serious threat is unbearable.

🐾 🐾 🐾

Yesterday, the eve of Halloween, I received this email from young Kirsty aka Harriet, the young poet with a cat called Merlin, who, she tells me, has just fully recovered from a near fatal car accident. She then, adorably, sends this email birthday card which is the first and only one that Gilly has received – oh, I am such a bad mother! ☹

– – –

From: Kirsty Wheeler
To: Marilyn Edwards
Sent: Sunday, October 30, 1:51 PM
Subject: Gilly's Birthday

To Gilly,

    HAPPY BIRTHDAY
From
Kirsty and Merlin

            >^-^< 'meow' Xxxxxxxxxxxxxxxx

Two days later I hear from Kate who, writing about her deceased cats, uses the magical phrase 'my

Three, plus a previous sealpoint, now all live in my heart'. Her writing moves me so much. I write back and she replies:

— — —

From: Kate Clarke
To: Marilyn Edwards
Sent: Tuesday, November 01, 9:31
Subject: Re: BRILLIANT!

Dear Marilyn,

The ashes of The Three are in their box in my bedroom and will be stirred into mine (not quite yet I hope!) before being sprinkled in a beautiful Glen in Scotland, where we spent three VERY happy years. Each one died in my arms.

Within a week of Harry's death 'The Computer at the Surgery' demanded I attend for my annual MOT and Doc asked, 'What's up, Kate?' I heard myself telling him that at that moment there was a huge jagged rock living just under my heart, but as this had happened before I knew that with time it would turn into a precious pearl. I waited for him to certify me, instead he agreed saying that the loss of an animal is a huge bereavement; we have to love animals to understand the hurt . . .

. . . I am honoured to have had them in my life. We are truly blessed, we who love The Glorious Cat.

Kate

That description of the pain of bereavement, which in time will turn into a precious pearl, even now, as I write, makes my eyes fill up. All of Kate's cats deserve more of a mention but for reasons of space I concentrate here on Harry. Kate writes:

HARRY: Cream Pointed Siamese, born 8 April 92, died 16 January 01. When I went to 'view' him, having been told his three sisters were chosen but he was left, I could understand why. In front of the large farmhouse fire curled up in a neat row lay three perfect little socks – his sisters. On a human knee lay the nearest thing I have seen to ET in my life. Long neck, HUGE feet, even bigger ears and the sapphire blue glorious eyes should have been swapped over as they appeared to be opposing each other. His coat at that stage was all pale cream, the glorious reddish caramel developed as he grew. Well, my dear, had to buy him, didn't I, no one else would – surely? Even my closest friends agreed, he was ugly. He grew into THE most dashing, gloriously handsome, big-hearted and kindly Gentleman ever. All three were fed together, Harry would sit back and wait for the girls to eat their fill before he approached! And a note for Michael, Harry was the best football player born, every article became a football . . . unless he decided that for a wee while it would be a rugby day! Sadly Harry developed thyroid problems, then my first experience of a cat suffering from the dreaded kidney problems. I will forever remember the Vet showing me the final results sheet saying, 'Unfortunately there is no Dialysis Treatment for animals.' Harry, a kind-hearted and true gentleman to his end, God bless him. I spent days clutching my red dressing gown – his favourite 'bed' . The girls missed him, so I had to get them over this by being 'normal'.

The time for Gilly's operation is now approaching and since early yesterday evening all four cats have been deprived of their food and have been restless most of the night as a result. Gilly is especially active, and so I weaken and arise. And then what a petitioning starts up! As I enter the kitchen to make some coffee Pushkin, Fannie and Titus all sit in a sad line, miaowing and making small plaintive moans. They are positioned in the precise places that the food bowls normally occupy. Their eyes are large and trusting and never leave me for a second. I bustle around and try not to hear or see them. Gilly, somewhat obligingly, has come down and positioned herself on top of the cat carrier that is to take her to the vet, so one way and the other the four felines have communicated emotional blackmail on full voltage. Gritting my teeth I grab Gilly and unceremoniously bundle her inside the carrier and off she and I go.

Why do I always feel this dreadful sense of doom? I have been extraordinarily lucky and nothing untoward has ever happened to any of my cats at any of the vets that I have taken them to, but I keep hearing such sad stories about things that go wrong under anaesthetic or in recovery. Recently, when Michael and I stayed in Bristol with our French Canadian friend France and her partner Mark, she showed me a picture of her very first cat, Smoky, a beautiful gentle long-haired black moggy, with a tiny white patch on his chest, and as she talked about him, her eyes misted over. At the time she is speaking of she was still living in Canada.

'I had to take Smoky to the vet because he had an eye-infection and the vet took the opportunity to give him a thorough examination and mentioned the poor state of his teeth at the time. Smoky was prescribed an antibiotic cream for his eyes and I then made an appointment to have his teeth cleaned.'

'How old was Smoky at this time?'

'He was ten years old and in fact I remember signing a paper where it was clearly stated that there was a risk for cats over the age of ten years old to be sedated, and I presumed this was a standard paper they were giving to everyone to cover themselves and I never thought that the risk was very high.' As she looks at the picture of Smoky, her eyes fill up, but she continues in a low, steady, voice:

'It was 13 October 1993, and I was at work. At around 5.00 p.m. the phone went and the vet, a woman, started to explain to me that Smoky had died at the very end of the cleaning process.'

'Was she contrite, did she sound upset?' I gasp, in horror.

'I think she was sincerely sad at what had happened. She described the whole cleaning process and told me how she had just extracted his rotten teeth and was preparing to take him out of anaesthesia, when his heart just stopped beating. She explained all the methods she tried to resuscitate him and gave me a tentative explanation for this accident. She thought he might have had a heart murmur and she could perform an autopsy if I wanted to know for sure. I said it didn't matter, it wouldn't bring him back. She also asked me if I wanted his body back, but I said she could dispose of it – have it incinerated. I had to go back to sign a few papers and she gave me the tooth she had extracted at the end. This I have kept as a memento of Smoky.' France looks at me, grinning, in her matter-of-fact way. I touch her hand sympathetically. Her voice changes:

'While I had kept my cool speaking to the vet, once I'd hung up, I remember sitting heavily on the chair near the phone, moaning out loud, "Mon chat est mort!" "Mon chat est mort!" A friend drove me back home and I remember crying my heart out all evening, all night and part of the next morning. I must have gone to work, but when I came back home I remember just frantically looking through the newspaper for kittens for sale. I found a place – the same friend drove me there – and the very next morning, a Friday, I came back home with a new kitten, who turned out to be the terrible Misty. My mourning of Smoky had been very intense but only lasted twenty-four hours or so.' France's use of the adjective 'terrible' in relation to Misty, who because of his bad behaviour ended up at the vet's almost monthly needing repairs of one kind or another, makes me laugh, but I gently suggest:

'You say "intense but only lasted twenty-four hours or so" . . . France, looking at you now, you still miss that dear little cat and you remember him with so much love and affection. Your grief lasted much longer than just those intense twenty-four hours of agony'. France in her turn laughs and adds:

'I do remember him very clearly. Smoky was rather a timid cat, especially with other cats, and he was very sweet. I can still picture my nephew Gabriel, then about two years old, carrying him upside down (rear paws and tail up in front of his face with Smoky's head and front paws trailing near the floor between Gaby's two spread legs as he was trying to bring Smoky to us without tripping on him). Held this way, the cat was almost as tall as him and sweet Smoky was not saying a thing about being mishandled like that, although he did climb up on some high furniture afterwards to get out of reach from Gaby when he finally let go of him. He was not an especially bright cat. More than once we ended up sitting on him because we had not seen him, and yet he always seemed to think we would never hurt him and would stop before we squashed him. He was that kind of cat with a total trust in humans, even young children, and in some terrible way you can't help but think, if it wasn't for me, he would still be alive. In the end, I feel it's "live and learn". I'm never going to have another of my cats operated on unless it is absolutely necessary and otherwise, I'll make sure they're checked annually so problems with teeth and all else can be prevented.' As I survey her sleek and content-looking cluster of cats, consisting of Apollo, Grippette, Spooky and Uni, I have no doubt at all that I am in the presence of a very well-nurtured group of felines.

In fact Kate, who emailed me at Halloween, told me that one of her beloved cats, Chloe died on 8 July 2003 after a dental cleaning operation 'went wrong' and she had to have her jaw wired:

The following seven weeks were HELL. You may think me totally and incurably nuts, but Chloe 'told' me with her eyes 'Come on, Mum, it's time, you must do it.' We went to the vet the next morning.

With all these gloomy thoughts in my mind I enter the surgery firmly gripping Gilly's cat-carrying cage, and as I announce myself at reception I notice another woman sitting down nursing a large long-haired cat in a cage on her knee, and while she is awaiting her turn to be seen, I realise that she is close to tears. She is called and leaves the cat in for surgery, and I long to ask her what her charge is there for, but her body language tells me she wants to be left alone, so I don't. As she has not taken the cage away with her I interpret that as probably positive. My turn arrives and after signing the dreaded 'consent form' for the operation and discussing the logistics of what is to happen, I leave Gilly to the tender mercies of the veterinary nurse Alison, who is very understanding. The whole process of surgery is so hard for the lads and lasses who have to carry it out, as they have to minister to the human end as well as the animals, and that is a hard call. The saintly Gerard phones me three hours later to tell me that Gilly has come round from the anaesthetic and he is happy with her progress. I feel a massive surge of relief. He is such a good vet, added to which he has a big heart, bless him. He remains concerned about her neurotic nibbling of her hair from her back legs and stomach, but as this is not life threatening, he says he will get back to me when he has spoken to a dermatologist friend, which he duly does. They are both pretty much in agreement that her initial hair loss had most likely been caused by a reaction to the itchiness caused by the harvest mites, but since then she has continued to nibble turning it into a psychogenic alopecia. 'Great,' I speculate gloomily, 'that should be easy to cure.'

The Yorkshire nature artist Richard Bell and his wife Barbara, whom Michael and I have met a couple of times over the last two years, arrive on their way back to Middlestown in Yorkshire from a holiday in the Lakes, just as I am about to depart to collect Gilly and bring her home. Richard does some superb sketches of Fannie, who is relaxing with Titus in the conservatory in her newfound freedom of a world without Gilly and they can be seen on his website, which is www.willowisland. co.uk and you then go into his Nature Diary for November 2005. In fact, he has written and illustrated many books, one of which I have sitting on my desk now, called *Rough Patch* which is breathtakingly beautiful, a really inspiring book packed with wonderful black and white sketches, crayon drawings and paintings and subtitled 'a sketchbook from the wilder side of the garden'. However, I have to leave Richard and Barbara in the capable hands of Michael while I set off through what seems like a never-ending wall of rain to collect the girl.

I jauntily bounce into the surgery to collect 'Black Magic' and Alison brings her into the consulting room in her carrier. I am gently pulled up short when I peer inside and find a very forlorn, somehow really small black ball hunched up, with her ears down like Yoda, looking very sorry for herself, indeed. As we talk I take in the exceptionally small neat scar that Gerard has managed in his deft surgery and the tiny area of fur that Alison has shaved off and am hugely grateful to them both for their joint effort in keeping the ever balding Gilly as intact as possible. After receiving some gentle post-operative advice from Alison, I bundle her up and put her in the car and drive the mile and a half home as carefully as possible. She is completely silent inside the cage until we come up the hill near the side of the house and about twenty feet away from the gate of the Coach House she lets out a long single but astonishingly loud wail, which I take to be a recognition sound at the smell of HOME. When I get her inside she is extremely wobbly on her legs so I carry her into the kitchen and let her eat and drink a little. The other cats watch her but keep their distance and at this stage there is no hissing from them at the smell of anaesthetic on her breath. She starts to walk towards the stairs and I follow nervously. As she starts to climb the first stair she is so wibbly-wobbly that I fear she will never make it, so I carry her up. I shut her in my study and stay in there myself. This is unheard of from the point of view of the other resident cats and I hear both Fannie and Titus making their protests outside the door.

'Sorry, guys, but this time it's her turn for TLC – you don't have to be in here, there is a fire lit downstairs, go on down', and eventually they do take themselves off. By early evening I reckon she is strong enough to take the presence of the other cats, so then I open the door and let them in, and she gets up and weakly tries to play with them. I have got an uncovered cat litter tray in my study to save her walking the stairs, but to my surprise she just lies in it for a while, so I swap it for a covered one from downstairs, which she eventually uses for the purpose it was intended. Titus is the only one to get really close to her and she gently hisses as she gets the first 'whiff' of anaesthetic, but that is all. Gilly considerably below par is a very strange phenomenon and tonight I would say she is definitely more knocked out than were either Fannie or Titus. She is a smaller framed cat than the other two girls so that may be why, or it could be the Bengal thing of being a 'drama queen'. She sleeps in the study on the armchair that is really the one that Titus and Fannie used to sleep in, but they both allow it unchallenged. We leave her there and eventually retire to our room to sleep. At about 4.15 a.m. I feel the gentle weight of Gilly jumping up on to our bed and she quietly nestles into my back. As I feel her relax against me I experience a huge twinge of guilt, but as I stroke her she purrs that all forgiving purr that cats have.

CHAPTER 23

Gilly has recovered well from her operation, and has calmed down when she is outside, her former rampaging far and wide is now, thank goodness, at an end, well for the moment at any rate. She continues to terrorise poor Fannie though, and Fannie has not regained any more confidence. If anything she is more uncertain than ever of where she stands in the hierarchy of the Coach House. Generally, it is more or less all right between Titus and Gilly. Sometimes there is just the shadow of irritation from Titus, but Gilly is respectful of Titus and at night on occasion they will both sleep on our bed, although not close to each other as would Fannie

and Titus, and that leads me to the night time ritual and how it is now. The glorious and superb thing about cats is that there is no standard status quo, there is no normal, there is no absolute. As soon as you think you know where a particular cat likes to lie, it will shun that place and find another much less suitable sleeping spot, and this goes equally for their loving rituals. There is no such thing as a 'usual' hello, or goodbye, or I love you. You may think there is, but it can change at a moment's notice. On the Coach House cats and their rituals, the current night-time ritual is that Gilly sleeps on the floor in the sitting-room in front of the fire, stretched out full length on the rug with the ease and territorial ownership of a small black Labrador. Titus and Fannie will have been curled up together

in the armchair in my study for most of the day
and/or evening, but as I turn out the lights, Titus
will come down and follow Michael and me up to
our room, and soon after that Pushkin will emerge
from whichever strange hiding place is his current
chosen spot. Gilly will stay in the sitting-room and
Fannie will stay in the study. We both stroke
Pushkin and Titus and then put out the lights.
Pushkin immediately leaves the room and returns
to an unknown place within the warmer part of the
house. Titus sometimes stays on our bed and
sometimes doesn't. After about an hour Gilly will
appear and lie stretched out next to either Michael

or me, depending upon her mood. But then sometimes she doesn't. Fannie never comes near us. Well, having said that, last night Fannie came in the middle of the night. None of the other cats was in our bedroom at the time. She quietly lay down on the bed between Michael and me and was there at dawn, and so for the first time in months she and I had our cuddle in the bathroom after my bath, but the sacred cuddle is now rare, although since writing this it has happened a few times, so again things are on the change a little perhaps?

George is ill. It was bound to happen that one of them would get ill sooner or later and it is poor little George. Yesterday, when I opened the hen coop and let them all out, I noticed that one of them was limping slightly, but I thought it wasn't serious. Then this morning I open the pop hole and she comes out last limping very badly. Every time she puts one leg near the ground she pulls it back as if she is touching hot bricks. As I am watching her she suddenly keels over and flumps down on her side. The other hens immediately gather round her and start to peck her, nastily, like they do. I phone the vet's and demand, rather rudely, to know if whoever is on duty knows anything about hens. It turns out that it is young Paul, who lives on a large mixed farm, and although only newly qualified he is brilliant with livestock of all kinds. On the phone there is loads of gloom about possibly Marek's disease, which rings all sorts of bells to do with the Herpes virus and the onset of tumours, but he says to bring her down and he'll have a look-see. After I have been waiting for a while the door opens and a young, good-looking farmer with a black Labrador with his tail in plaster comes in and sits next to me. We are both there as Saturday morning emergencies. His Lab sniffs inquiringly at my solid-sided cat carrier and the young man says:

'What's wrong with your cat?'

'It's not a cat.' Suddenly abashed, I go quiet.

'What on earth is in there, then?'

'A hen.'

'A hen? A hen did you say? But for goodness sake you would only have paid a couple of quid for that and think what the bill at the end of this lot will be!' I laugh, and mumble something about the quality of life, but as he continues to tease me I protest:

'But hey, you wouldn't have ignored the plight your dog was in, even though the vet's bills might eventually mount up to more than you paid for him, would you?'

'Well, no, but he's a dog. Oh, alright, fair enough then.'

It all becomes slightly embarrassing as it's my turn first and I take her into the surgery and by this time – it had been really cold overnight, the temperature had dropped at one point to −5°C – George is beginning to perk up a bit and look quite bright-eyed again in the unaccustomed heat of the car and now the warm surgery. Paul asks me if I know her weight and, of course, I haven't a clue, so we have to weigh the cat carrier with her in it and then, while his young assistant holds her, without her in it and all this time the young man and his dog are looking on askance as we pass him to get to the scales. Paul examines her and pronounces her to be free of the dreaded Marek's disease.

'I am fairly confident that it is a neuromuscular injury she has suffered. She has somehow damaged herself, flying into something possibly.' With that he deftly injects her with Rimadyl which is used for arthritis in dogs. The reason he needs to know her weight is so that he doesn't overdose her, and as he plunges the needle into her she never makes a sound. We pack her up into her cage and I sneak past the young farmer wishing him luck with his dog. He grunts, but smiles back. That one felt like a baptism of fire. It is the first time I have run the gauntlet of a vet's surgery with a hen.

I get George back to her little paddock and open the cat carrier, and to my complete amazement she runs, yes, actually runs across the yard to join her coop-mates. She appears to be totally recovered. This time they just welcome her back and don't peck at her. As I am watching my little flock I suddenly become aware of them all switching their fixated gaze from me – always along with Michael a good touch for a treat of some kind – to the sky behind my head. I swing round to see what they are watching – they have gone completely silent – and there I see two huge buzzards[54] riding the thermals in slow, large circles. To begin with they are over the woods behind the house, then they glide over

---

[54] Buteo buteo

the house and now they are directly overhead. As they get ever closer I can hear that haunting 'pee-uuu' noise they mew to each other. The hens appear almost hypnotised but also a little apprehensive. Would a buzzard seriously be a predator for a large hen, I wonder? But also how do these hens, who have only known Maurice Jackson's farm near Keighley and more recently Hutton Roof, have such a finely honed instinct that they can recognise a possible predator so quickly and absolutely? We do get buzzards here, year-round, so perhaps it is from their time here and, for sure, a small chick would be vulnerable. Shortly after this sighting, rather disconcertingly I receive the following email from Mary White about her Bengal cat Purdie, which sets my alarm bells going on the subject of buzzards and not just in the context of chickens:

From: Mary White
To: Marilyn Edwards
Sent: Sunday, December 10, 11:11 AM
Subject: Re: Purdie the Immortal Bengal

Marilyn, let me tell you quickly about another Purdie life being used – I think she has 19 not 9.

During the summer Richard was doing some work in the garden – it was a lovely day and Purdie was just hanging around. Directly to the rear of the garden we have acre upon acre of farm fields, mainly used for hay, and a haven for little creatures such as voles, shrews, etc., and BUZZARDS–bloody great enormous birds that circle around looking for mice, that have a wing span of several feet.

On this day, Richard was working and Purdie was sitting on the path. Richard suddenly looked up the length of the path to see a buzzard swooping directly towards Purdie, claws and feet extended for the catch! Purdie just sat there looking completely unbothered. There was no time for Richard to do anything apart from watch in horror. It came down and the ONLY thing that stopped it taking her was that the 2 chimney pots on the path with my fuchsias in it seemed to be in its flight path and it had to swerve to miss them and misjudged its angle on poor Purdie, still sitting there nonchalantly! Richard said it came within inches of him and her . . .

So she is very unlucky this cat, or perhaps very lucky?

Love,

Mary

PS In case you ask, I did say to Richard that Purdie is quite a small cat (very small for a Bengal) and that perhaps the buzzard thought she was a large rabbit . . . or maybe we are kidding ourselves. Birds of prey, after all, do have the proverbial 'eyes like a hawk' and are supposed to be able to see for miles with 20/20 perfect vision! You'll remember Purdie's colouring, tabby with different kinds of browns and blacks.

I should mention that Mary White was the breeder from whom I acquired Pushkin, and I remember well, three years ago, meeting Purdie, who is a predominantly brown and black tabby. I then lost touch, and thanks to Ruth, who emailed me about her Pushkin earlier this year, we are now in contact again. Some time ago she told me the remarkable story of how Purdie had gone missing for ten days and when she did arrive back she was severely lame, with one hind leg held up from the ground. She was assumed by the vet to have been run over and by the time she hobbled home she was close to starving. On examination she had a severely fractured hip joint and following surgery was prescribed cage rest for a whole month. For a Bengal and her human carers that is such a long time! Imagine the noise. Her leg was nerve damaged, and the vet and everyone else said she would never regain the use of it. Mary massaged the leg every night and Purdie kept pulling the leg away; Mary persevered in spite of Purdie's protestations and, nearly four months after the accident, Purdie is now walking almost perfectly. When she wants to run she still uses the three legs, but can walk on all four. The good that has come from all of this is that Purdie is now a changed cat. She, who used to go off regularly for days at a time, now never goes out at night and she never strays far from the house, even in daylight.

Kevin Dean, whom I first had contact with two years ago, is a young composer, instrumentalist and cabaret performer who confesses to spending 'all my wages on cat food for the strays when I work abroad'. When I first knew him he told me, with much excitement, that he was about to move house and was yearning to adopt two cats from the Country Cat Shelter in Lowestoft.

'There are many cats in the cat shelter, but there are two older girls with sadness in their eyes. Nobody wants them. They are overweight. I will get them sorted out. Lovely girls they are, Marilyn.' These two sisters had had a tough time because a couple who had originally cared for them, split up and, unable to look after them any more, took the cats to the shelter, then made up again and took the cats back home, and then sadly split up again, so the cats were returned to the shelter. When Kevin first sees them they have been in the shelter for five months, getting sadder by the week. He commits to sharing his home with these girls and names them Abbey Moon and Angel Moon. He visits them regularly while he is waiting to move, some times as often as three times a week for the next couple of months.

'Also I would "do the rounds" and give fuss to all the other cats. Kittens and pregnant mothers would come and go. The three-year-old dark tortie "Trixie" was still there. She was a very nervous cat. She had been at the shelter for the same amount of time as the sisters. Trixie was found in a barn mothering her litter and was often seen going out hunting with a fox. How could I not give her a home too? I told Elaine (who runs the shelter) that Trixie could come to Pixie Cottage as well. I re-named her Petal Rose. She walks like a fox.'

When Kevin first gets them back home Abbey and Angel immediately start investigating the cottage. Petal just hides under the kitchen table. Everything goes wonderfully well at the beginning and they all eat and learn to use the litter trays as Kevin hopes:

'I put their trays in the utility room. A cat flap leads from the kitchen to the utility. And for the first few days there were no problems. They knew where the toilet was and they seemed to be very content! But . . . one night I watched Petal go through the cat flap to the toilet. Within seconds she was back in the kitchen! She was one very shaken cat. What on earth happened? I just thought it was Petal being silly. A few minutes later Abbey wandered into the utility. Déjà vu! She zoomed back in too! What a commotion. I grabbed my keys and ventured into the utility. Nothing! I then opened the utility door to the garden. I had a wander around. Nothing. The outer utility door is partly patterned glass. Was it a fox peering through? Or maybe another cat? Or what? The cats remained nervous and shaky, including Angel, who hadn't even gone through the cat flap at the time. Petal hid herself. The two sisters just sat and nervously look towards the utility area. I went to bed. Petal normally sleeps on my office chair in the studio. Angel kips in the corner of the studio. And Abbey is Daddy's girl who sleeps on my bed. The night of the utility scare, Petal hid all night. Angel and Abbey slept in their usual places. The utility was not used again. The next morning I found a deposit on the rug in the front room. That following day I never heard the flap go again, but they just kept staring at it nervously!'

In fact, Kevin never does find out what it is that

so upset all three cats, but they do settle down and become very contented cats in their new-found freedom with someone they can trust. As the time approaches for them to be let out of doors I become fretful, because their former traffic-sense may have been dulled and also for Petal Rose who is a near feral cat, will she revert to her wild ways?

He does let them out, of course, and they are fine and become visibly happier and more relaxed, as they realise they are properly 'home'. Wonderfully, the nervous Petal becomes especially close to Angel, who looks out for her. All three of them get on remarkably well.

I continue to follow the tales of Kevin's cats with some interest. One day Kevin asks me if he ever told me about his 'vortex experience'.

'It first happened a few years ago. I arrived home from doing a cabaret show, totally sober. I lay back on the sofa with a glass of wine and put on the TV to catch the last half hour of a Bond film. Tigger-Mu-Mu was on the coffee table between me and the TV. She was facing away from me towards the large window with the curtains drawn. Tiggs was having a good wash in true Mogology style.

Suddenly something caught my eye way left of the TV against the curtains. I looked and it was unbelievable . . . a swirling purple/blue vortex. That's the only way I can describe it. But what caught my eye even more was Tiggs, stuck in mid-wash, looking at the vortex. This vortex looked like something was trying to manifest. The episode lasted only a few seconds. When the vortex disappeared Tiggs continued to look at the space for a few seconds longer and then carried on washing. This sent shivers down my spine because Tiggs was not influenced by me at all and yet she clearly saw what I was seeing. It wasn't caused by a light shining through the window because the bungalow is in a cul-de-sac with no passing traffic; it has a large front garden, and thick curtains! What I saw was in the room.'

I am disconcerted by this and ask Kevin lots of questions. He says that he only experienced the 'vortex' once but on several occasions he saw a 'ghost' cat and so, he discovers recently, did his mother. However, both of them only saw it in this particular bungalow. It would be visible to him out of the corner of his eye and it would seem to be walking in that way that cats do and that in some strange way it looked like Tigger-Mu-Mu, which is odd as she was alive then, but the moment he turned round and looked at it square on it would fade.

'Sometimes I wondered if it was Barnaby Lilly, my first cat, but she wasn't a tabby. Sometimes when I saw it, I would then see Tiggs kipping on the chair. Could it be Tiggs astral projecting?'

All I feel able to offer is the Bard of Avon's immortal: 'There are more things in heaven and earth, Horatio, than are dreamt of in your philosophy.'

One day Kevin astonishes me by telling me that having read *The Cats of Moon Cottage* and been roused by the account of the deaths of Otto and Septi, he has written a piece of music to their memory. The track is called 'Otto and Septi's Tune' and it features on a CD called Mogology: *Music for Cats and Cat Lovers.*[54] When he sent it to me he said:

' "Otto and Septi's Tune" tells a story, musically.

---

[54] Mogology by EOL/KDM Productions Cat No: MOG7318

The general "hook" is their tune. The two electric guitars are the two cats: the main guitar being Septi and the replying and harmonizing guitar being Otto moving her way into Septi's life. Often the two guitars are played together in harmony expressing the two cats in harmony together. The slightly haunting sinister middle section represents the two deaths; firstly Otto's, then Septi's, and then it's back to that main hook – their tune celebrating their lives and them being together again in cat heaven.'

When I first heard it, it made me cry. Three-quarters of the way through there are three very subtle heart-stopping distant cat calls over a near purr. The music is very beautiful. I suspect that that first book moved Kevin so much because of the experiences he had with his cat Barnaby Lilly, to whom he pays tribute with the piece of music, also on this CD, called 'The Tortoiseshell'. Barnaby Lilly was the very first cat in Kevin's life and was a beautiful white-fronted tortoiseshell. She became ill with tumours and Kevin, heart-broken, had to have her put to sleep. Tigger-Mu-Mu, a Cypress tabby, was his next cat. She had thyroid problems, but the pills his vet gave her seemed to sort her out. But slowly the passage of time took its toll on his little tabby cat.

'Tiggs would have days when she wouldn't eat at all and would just kip. These days started to happen more often. On the morning of 6 June last year I walked into the lounge and she was having trouble breathing. I knew this was it. I stayed with her and she died within half an hour. I think she was just waiting for me to get out of bed to say goodbye. She was always a spoilt cat, and still is! She is buried under a fountain feature with mist and lights that I bought for her the next day.' Kevin's music for Tiggs is a haunting melody called 'Purrs in Heaven'.

CHAPTER 24

Annabel comes across this morning for a quick chat and tells me, laughingly, that her brother Henry, a retired farmer, told her I mustn't – just mustn't – kiss the chickens. She says that she has been told to come and tell me this as it has been issued as a serious government warning.

'I mean honestly, Marilyn, as if you would.' I grin sheepishly. The truth is that all the hens are now extremely tame and will allow both Michael and me to pick them up and give them cuddles, and as most of them jump on to the wall when we go in to see them, they greet us at head height. Not that I actually do kiss them, beaks are strangely off-putting, but if they wanted to kiss us, or we them, it would be very easy so to do. The hens are now laying eggs daily and they are a beautiful deep brown colour with dark yellow yolks and truly delicious.

Annabel and Richard are off to Australia to spend Christmas with their daughter and just before they go they give us an enchanting present. It is a small glass pot of honey, the size and shape that Pooh Bear was especially fond of and the colour of the honey it contains is pure gold. Around the pot, designed by the fair hand of Richard himself, is a white label with the words:

AMBROSIA
Food of the Gods
from
Hutton Roof

Underneath this bold statement is a copy of Shepherd's wonderful drawing of Pooh hanging on to the string of a balloon surrounded by faintly hostile bees and underneath the drawing the phrase 'You never can tell with bees'.

As I thank Annabel effusively I observe:

'But they never swarmed on us this summer, they behaved impeccably.'

'Ah, but you never can tell,' she affirms.

Eating the food of the gods from Hutton Roof spread thickly on buttered bread is truly divine.

🐧 🐧 🐧

In this book I have attempted to observe and record the lives of the cats in the Coach House as accurately as possible and here, as the year end is reached, I give the reader a quick update.

Gilly has not only recovered well from her operation but also from her allergy to the harvest mite; all her glossy black fur has grown back on her legs and her tummy and over her scar and she looks sleek and shiny and well. Even her wonky whiskers are better than they have been before, although they will never be anything to write home about!

Fannie and Gilly continue to be full of aggression or fear towards each other, although on some days several hours will pass without any sign of tension between them and each day that happens I hope against hope that the dynamics of their relationship is sorted out, but in reality I don't think a day has passed without there being some explosive outburst between them both. Fannie has just learned recently how to be brave enough to come into the bathroom in the morning for her cuddle, and I think that is helping her; it is certainly helping me.

Pushkin and Gilly are friendly in a mutually fun-loving, chasing sort of way, although they never lie together. The only one Pushkin lies near is Titus, but then that is true of Gilly: she will lie with Titus too, but none of the others. Pushkin spends more of the day awake now, playing with Gilly and checking out where she is. He does seem to be quite infatuated by her. Gilly enjoys being with Pushkin and rampages around with him more than any of the others, and they always 'kiss' each other when they meet up in the hallway, or anywhere else. But of all the cats it is Titus whose company Gilly actively seeks out and, it appears to me, whose approval she seeks.

The bond has considerably strengthened again between Titus and Fannie and Titus to some extent protects Fannie from Gilly. They spend much time each day lying together in the chair in my study now, and Fannie seems to gain reassurance from this.

A small drama has just unfolded before us, which indicates something I had not previously known about the relationship between Titus and Fannie. Michael and I are sitting on a sofa in front of the fire watching television and Gilly is lying very close to the stove on the floor stretched out. Titus is resting, in a slightly uncomfortable-looking pose, on the empty sofa. Fannie comes down from upstairs and peers through the banisters to check where Gilly is lying, sees she is stretched out with her eyes closed and so squeezes between a pair of the balustrades, along the back of Titus's sofa and down into the kitchen to eat. Gilly hearing her eating, gets up, stretches, throws her one of her stares and, with all the normal accompanying hissing and spitting, chases her with great force back upstairs to my study. Gilly then saunters back down as she always does after she has 'despatched' Fannie in this way. Titus gets up off the sofa, slowly stretches, and walks over to Gilly who is sitting upright looking at the fire. Gilly turns her head round to look at Titus who then hits Gilly, three times rapidly, each one a really hard thwack with her front foot and then, without a backward glance, Titus goes upstairs to find Fannie. She rather disconcertingly has an expression on her face like my father's when he was in a rage.

'Did you see that, Michael?'

'Yes, I did. She did that for Fannie'.

'Do you *really* think that is why?'

'There was absolutely no other reason why she'd have just got up and clocked Gilly like that, it must've been because she didn't like what Gilly did to Fannie.' I look across at Gilly. She is looking into the fire quietly. I guess she is thinking, but what *is* it that she's thinking?

To complete this tableau Pushkin meanders into the room via the window from the conservatory courtesy of the cats' scratching post, climbs across the top of the bookcase, walks over Michael and me and our sofa and subsides gracefully in a leggy sprawl across the coffee table between us and the television like a small Russian Blue Emperor. He is now obscuring half of the screen from us but he, on the other hand, has an excellent view. The clock ticks, quietly and the logs crackle, merrily. I sigh, happily. I reckon this is as good as it gets with the four Coach House cats.

POSTCRIPT

With the completion of this fourth book continuing the story which started with *The Cats of Moon Cottage*, my editor and I feel it is now time to give the Moon Cottage/Coach House cats a rest, but we thank you, the reader, wholeheartedly for your support and encouragement.

As all cat lovers will know, and as some of the stories in this book illustrate, sharing your life with a cat can be pure joy, although there may be the odd trial too. Sometimes one of the rewards is being cared for in return with such intensity that it is life-enhancing. If you are lucky, loving and being loved by cats can lift you on to another plane.

I have felt both privileged and grateful to the many readers who have contacted me with their feedback on the books as they have read them and who have chosen to share their wonderful and sometimes very funny stories about their cats with me. Sadly, due to lack of space, I have been able to share only a few of these stories through this book, so I am now setting up a page on my website www.thecatsofmooncottage.co.uk which will be called 'Cat Story 1, 2, 3, etc.' The stories will remain accessible from the home page for a few weeks after which they will then be archived, and accessible through my website archive.

Marilyn Edwards

ACKNOWLEDGEMENTS

The author and publishers are grateful for permission to reproduce the following copyright material:

France Bauduin: Sketch of Harriet and Chester, reproduced on p. 161 (© 2005)
Doreen Dann: The Kitten House or Why Not a Black One? (© 2000)
Harriet Garside: A Wild Hack (©2004)
Anne Huntington: Tales of a Postmistress (© December 1995)
Beth Loft: Woolgathering: Ramblings of a woman who really ought to know better – Treacle archive blog (© 2005)

My cat books owe their very existence to the following three people. To Judith Longman at Hodder I proffer my deep gratitude for her skilful editorial sensibility, for believing in my books and for fighting their corner. To Peter Warner my heartfelt thanks for his unique and superb illustrations all of which have added another dimension to the story contained within each book and which have made the books very special and to my own dear Michael my loving recognition of his forebearance and encouragement in every way which made it possible for me to write them in the first place.

To Janice Swanson and Kate Cooper and their teams at Curtis Brown my ongoing appreciation for their continued championship of both Peter and me throughout the publication of these four books to find a wider audience, and I would like especially to thank Cecilia Moore, Sandy Waldron, Victoria Bullock, Catherine Worsley, those brilliant sales reps, Jean Whitnall and all those in sales who work with her and I would further like to extend that thanks to Bookpoint and to the many staff of the following chains who so magnificently supported and believed in the earlier books including Ottakar's, Waterstones, Borders and Books Etc, Amazon, WH Smith and those wonderful independents all around the country together with their supporting wholesalers.

The following people have all, in some particular way, made their own contribution to this current book and to them a special word of thanks. They are Brian Alderson, John and Margaret Armistead, Sue Baker, France Bauduin, Richard Bell, Catherine, Elizabeth, Hilary, Peter and Phil Bull, Claire and Hugh Carrington, Annabel and Richard Challenor, Anthony and Jacky Chaplow, Melissa Chinchillo, Jane Cholmeley, Kate Clarke, Doreen Dann, Kevin Dean, Damian, Johnny, John and Oliver Dugdale, Sue Fallon, Shirani Fernando-Bradford, Harriet Garside aka Kirsty, Christopher, Sue, Alex and Adam Gordon, Alex, Jeff, Karen, Lesley and Neil Hilton, Catherine and Ray Hughes, Anne Huntington, Maurice and Ruth Jackson, Kalyacitta, Marje Klokow, Rita Lawson, Beth Loft, Geoffrey Moorhouse, Anette Nyberg, Emma Parker, Amanda Picknell, Sue and Richard Prickett, Doreen and Thomas Raw, Elizabeth and

Ian Rooke, David Stubbs, Vajragupta, Caroline Wallace and Nathan Richardson, Ann Waller, Ruth Weinberg, Mary White, Shirley Windmill and a huge thank you to Gerard Winnard and his doughty team especially Paul (Smith), Ben, Alison, Liz and Cathy and of course a massive thank you to the cats Fannie, Titus, Pushkin and Gilly truly without whom . . .

Finally a profound thank you is of course due to the thousands of cat lovers out there who have been kind enough to buy the first book and who then return to buy the next one. THANK YOU!

Marilyn Edwards

To contact either author or illustrator, details are as follows:

Marilyn Edwards: The Coach House, Hutton Roof, Kirkby Lonsdale, Cumbria, LA6 2PG

Marilyn Edwards' email: Mooncottagecats@hotmail.com

Marilyn Edwards' website: www.thecatsofmooncottage.co.uk

Peter Warner: Peter Warner's Studio, Hillside Road, Tatsfield, Kent, TN16 2NH

Peter Warner's email: thestudio@peterwarner.com

Peter Warner's website: www.peterwarner.com

Animal *Health* Trust

The Feline Unit at the Animal Health Trust

The Feline Unit is a part of the small animal clinic within the AHT dedicated to the care of cats with various internal medicine problems. The AHT is one of the UK's foremost veterinary charities undertaking a wide range of treatments for sick animals that are referred to its clinic, but also undertaking substantial work into investigating the causes of disease and new techniques in the treatment and management of disease. The AHT is one of the few institutes to dedicate resources specifically to the care of cats, and it relies heavily on donations to support its ongoing work.

The contact details for the Feline Unit at the Animal Health Trust are: Lanwades Park, Kentford, Newmarket, Suffolk, CB8 7UU, UK
Tel (+44) 8700 502424

Dr Andy Sparkes, BvetMed,PhD,
DipECVIM, MRCVS, RCVS